BCIM

ANTHOLO[G]

WITH GREAT

2

WITH
GREAT
PLEASURE

WITH GREAT PLEASURE

VOLUME II

*An Anthology of Poetry and Prose from
the BBC Radio 4 Programme*

EDITED BY ALEC REID

HUTCHINSON
LONDON   SYDNEY   AUCKLAND   JOHANNESBURG

© Foreword and Selection Alec Reid 1988

First published in Great Britain in 1988 by Hutchinson, an imprint of
Century Hutchinson Ltd, Brookmount House, 62–65 Chandos Place,
London WC2N 4NW

Century Hutchinson Australia Pty Ltd
89–91 Albion Street, Surry Hills, NSW 2010, Australia

Century Hutchinson New Zealand Ltd
PO Box 40-086, Glenfield, Auckland 10, New Zealand

Century Hutchinson South Africa (Pty) Ltd
PO Box 337, Bergvlei, 2012, South Africa

British Library Cataloguing in Publication Data

With great pleasure.
   Vol. 2
   1. Great Britain. Radio programmes: With great pleasure – Scripts –
   Collections
   I. Reid, Alec, *1943–*
   791.44'72

   ISBN 0 09 173614 5

Photoset by Rowland Phototypesetting Ltd
Bury St Edmunds, Suffolk
Printed and bound in Great Britain by
Anchor Brendon Ltd, Tiptree, Essex

CONTENTS

CONTENTS

ACKNOWLEDGEMENTS

Every Day in Every Way by KIT WRIGHT reprinted by permission of Tessa Sayle Agency

Letter to Sandor Ferenczi by SIGMUND FREUD reprinted by permission of Hogarth Press

Selected Letters and *The Ascent of Parnassus Made Easy* by DYLAN THOMAS reprinted by permission of David Higham Associates Ltd

The Ghost reprinted by permission of the Literary Trustees of WALTER DE LA MARE and the Society of Authors as their representative

The Flight From Bootle and *Blame the Vicar* by John Betjeman reprinted by permission of John Murray (Publishers) Ltd

Tarantella by HILAIRE BELLOC reprinted by permission of A. D. Peters & Co. Ltd

The Life of the Bee by MAETERLINCK trans Alfred Sutro reprinted by permission of George Allen and Unwin

Doggerel About Old Days, *Memoirs of a Fox-Hunting Man* and *The General* by SIEGFRIED SASSOON reprinted by permission of George Sassoon

Symptom Recital by DOROTHY PARKER reprinted by permission of Laurence Pollinger Ltd

Extract by ATHENE SEYLER from *The RADA Graduate's Keepsake and Handbook* reprinted by permission of RADA

Extract from the Diary of HUGH WALPOLE reprinted by permission of M. L. R. Ltd

Extract from *Duet for One* by TOM KEMPINSKI reprinted by permission of Anthony Sheil Associates Ltd

Extract from *One for the Road* by WILLY RUSSELL reprinted by permission of Margaret Ramsay Ltd

On a Tide of Murder by PHILIP NORMAN reprinted by permission of A. D. Peters & Co. Ltd

We Need a Star by MICHAEL BURNETT reproduced by permission of the author

The Tower by W. B. YEATS reproduced by permission of A. P. Watt Ltd on behalf of Michael Yeats and Macmillan London Ltd

Funeral Blues and *Miss Gee* by W. H. AUDEN reprinted by permission of Faber and Faber Ltd

The Ruin trans KEVIN CROSSLEY-HOLLAND reproduced by permission of Deborah Rogers Ltd

The Eternal Order by EDWARD GRUBB reprinted by permission of Heckford, Norton & Co.

The Happy Hour by SYLVIA LIND reprinted by permission of Victor Gollancz Ltd

Close of Play by ALAN MILLER reprinted by permission of Hodder & Stoughton Ltd

Bagpipe Music by LOUIS MACNEICE published by Faber and Faber Ltd and reproduced by permission of David Higham Associates Ltd

The Oxford Hysteria of English Poetry from 'Ride the Nightmare' by ADRIAN MITCHELL reprinted by permission of Jonathan Cape Ltd

Extract from *The Dog Beneath the Skin* by W. H. AUDEN & CHRISTOPHER ISHERWOOD reprinted by permission of Curtis Brown Ltd

may i feel said he by E. E. CUMMINGS reprinted by permission of Jonathan Cape Ltd

Introduction to a Science of Mythology by JUNG & KERENYI trans R. F. C. Hull reprinted by permission of Routledge & Kegan Paul plc

Like Men Betrayed by FREDERICK RAPHAEL reprinted by permission of A. P. Watt Ltd

Plain Words by ERNEST GOWERS reprinted by permission of HMSO

Who Am I? by DIETRICH BONHOEFFER reprinted by permission of SCM Press

Code Poem for the French Resistance by LEO MARKS reprinted by permission of Big Ben Music Ltd

Extract from *People of Providence* by TONY PARKER reprinted by permission of Anthony Sheil Associates Ltd

SPITTING IMAGE BOOK *Dear Mr Eggnogge* © SUE TOWNSEND

Imaginings by ROBERT GITTINGS reprinted by permission of Secker and Warburg Ltd

FOREWORD

From the beginning there was talk that Century Hutchinson might wish to publish a second volume based on Radio 4's 'With Great Pleasure'. For that very reason, when compiling Volume I, I had to discipline myself not just to think in terms of producing a 'best of' collection, but to put some of my favourite editions to one side. Fortunately most of the programmes from the first in 1970 to the one I recorded earlier this week have been entertaining, with many including unusual pieces which reveal much about the guest people chosen to offer their favourite poetry and prose to the assembled audience. Inevitably, with the passing of time and the fickleness of public interest, certain names had lost their lustre, a few programmes must have sounded better on the air than they read on the page and a few more just did not capture my imagination. As to the latter I merely claimed the anthologist's privilege of leaving out anything which did not give *me* pleasure. Some of those omitted from Volume I were friends of mine and here I could only carry out the anthologist's duty of presenting what I hoped was a balanced selection regardless of personal preference. I am happy to be able to include them now.

In the Foreword to our first volume I mentioned that we had just recorded an edition of 'With Great Pleasure' with Peter Pears. Sadly, since then he has died. He will be fondly remembered in his beloved Aldeburgh and by friends all over the world. To all of us his voice will remain familiar through his many recordings with Benjamin Britten. These, along with the festival he helped to create, will be his legacy. Nevertheless, it gives me some satisfaction to add to it in some small degree by including part of his programme here.

Reading through recent 'With Great Pleasure' scripts, I am pleased to note a decline of interest in 'The Old Vicarage, Grantchester'. No one has included it for at least two years now. John Betjeman is chosen as often as he ever was: it is rare for a programme not to contain a poem of his – often a presenter tries to squeeze in two or three. However, in the interests of variety I tend to discourage having more than one piece by any author. Thomas Hardy and Robert Browning would certainly feature in any 'With Great Pleasure' hit parade, whilst Jane Austen would probably top the charts as the most quoted novelist. Although all are included in this book, I have not been over zealous in obeisance. One of the things that makes the programme of such continuing interest to the listeners is the choice of unfamiliar and unexpected material. For that reason Jane Austen is represented here not by *Persuasion* or *Pride and Prejudice*, but a rarely-seen piece written when she was a young girl.

This time there is no unpublished fragment by Geoffrey Chaucer, but there *is* unpublished Alan Bleasdale, especially written for the programme. Perhaps even more heartwarming are a couple of poems presented as an act of friendship, one to Heather Couper by Michael Burnett, the other to Ian Wallace by Robert Gittings – and jolly good they are too. There is also a poem by W. H. Auden which he tried to suppress because he thought it too shocking.

So, if your taste inclines to the sentimental you will find items enough to moisten at least two hankies. There are also pieces of savagery and wit, which express a profound distaste for life. However there are many more whose essence is the joy of being alive. It is that which in the end makes 'With Great Pleasure' such a genuine pleasure for so many listeners. As broadcasts are by their nature here today and gone tomorrow, it is my pleasure to offer this more permanent reminder of such a popular series.

Alec Reid
April 1988

DANNIE ABSE

1984

Before I moved to Bristol from London, Dannie Abse and I regularly used to have lunch together at an Italian restaurant just around the corner from the Middlesex Hospital where he worked. He always ordered the same dish, a Pizza Napoli without the anchovy. 'After all,' he argued, 'if you come to a pizza place you really ought to order a pizza.' It was a form of gastronomic logic I was unable to follow, but it was the only part of being with him that was in any way routine. He is a witty and clever conversationalist, always ready to startle with a fresh idea. I didn't have the pleasure of producing his 'With Great Pleasure', but at the time of writing have just arranged for him to be the subject of some 'Time for Verse' programmes. It will be a happy opportunity to work with him again and lunch is already on the agenda. So, no doubt, is the Pizza Napoli without the anchovy.

At the rehearsal of this programme I heard someone say, 'Is he a real doctor?' I should have worn a tie. I became a doctor because of my eldest brother Wilfred who, not long after he had qualified as a physician, returned to our house in Cardiff to find me uselessly pushing a saucer of milk towards our sick cat. Merlin lay motionless on the carpet, his eyes staring at nothing. Was Merlin dying? 'I wouldn't mind being a vet,' I said.

I was a fourteen-year-old schoolboy, who wanted to be a concert pianist, an assassin that did for Hitler, a crooner like Bing Crosby, a boxer like Tommy Farr, a jockey like Gordon Richards, a racing driver like Sir Malcolm Campbell, the best centre forward

Cardiff City ever had, the fastest wing-threequarter capped for Wales, the greatest opening bat in Glamorgan's history. Maybe, in my spare time, I could become a reasonable vet?

'Better to become a doctor,' Wilfred had replied, 'like me, like so many of your cousins – like Uncle Max, like Uncle Joe.'

So, unselfish, I gave up all my ambitions and became a mere doctor. I say mere, because I've known a few in my life. My Uncle Max, apart from believing in the efficacy of modern drugs, believes powerfully in the power of suggestion. So did Dr Coué – whose theories of auto-suggestion apparently became a craze during the 1920s. On his recommendation hordes of people woke up in the morning to intone, 'Every day, in every way, I grow better and better.' A poet acquaintance of mine, Christopher . . . Kit . . . Wright, obviously tried out Dr Coué's recommendation himself.

Every Day in Every Way
KIT WRIGHT

When I got up this morning
I thought the whole thing through:
Thought, Who's the hero, the man of the day?
Christopher, it's you.

With my left arm I raised my right arm
High above my head:
Said, Christopher, you're the greatest.
Then I went back to bed.

I wrapped my arms around me,
No use counting sheep.
I counted legions of myself
Walking on the deep.

The sun blazed on the miracle,
The blue ocean smiled:
We like the way you operate,
Frankly, we like your style.

Dreamed I was in a meadow,
Angels singing hymns,

2

Fighting the nymphs and shepherds
Off my holy limbs.

A girl leaned out with an apple,
Said, You can taste for free.
I never touch the stuff, dear,
I'm keeping myself for me.

Dreamed I was in heaven,
God said, Over to you,
Christopher, you're the greatest!
And Oh, it's true, it's true!

I like my face in the mirror,
I like my voice when I sing.
My girl says it's just infatuation –
I know it's the real thing.

Doctors can be fair game for satirists. But what about patients?
Sometimes they can be incredible. I recall one chap who was all in
a dither because his wife had just had a baby. To keep him quiet I
suggested he went out to buy mother and child a present. He
returned with flowers for his wife and a bar of chocolate for his
newborn son. 'I don't think . . .' I began. 'Don't worry, doctor,'
he interrupted me blithely, 'it's *milk* chocolate.' It was a very
big bar. Ignorant he was, stingy he was not, unlike Jimmy
MacDougal:

A bugler called Jimmy MacDougal
Found ingenious ways to be frugal.
He learned how to sneeze
In various keys
Thus saving the price of a bugle.

Two of the pleasures of the morning for me are buttered toast and
letters. If one or two real letters don't lie on the mat in the
morning I feel the day hasn't truly begun. I'm glad, though, that
these days I don't receive letters from one who called himself 'The
Master'. Some years ago, whenever I appeared in print, published a book, did a broadcast, I would receive, on a tatty scrap of
paper, a letter signed 'The Master'. These anonymous letters
were in no way abusive. On the contrary, they were usually

appreciative and, moreover, literary, finely composed. They puzzled me very much. Naturally I looked at the postmark. They came from a small town west of London. But knowing that didn't help. I received The Master's letters, usually written on blue-lined paper, for the best part of a decade. Indeed, when I published something I began to *wait* for The Master's response. One Friday my wife happened on a letter in the *New Statesman* written by a novelist whom I shall now call 'Tony'. 'Didn't you used to know Tony a little when you were a student?' my wife asked. 'Look at the address he's writing from.' It was from that same small town west of London. Tony was older than me – he'd had several novels published when I first met him and was much better known than he is now. Anyway, I took a chance and wrote to him:

Dear Tony,
Thank you for all those constructive and interesting letters you've sent me over the years.
Best Wishes
Dannie

The reply came back immediately:

Dear Dannie,
You've found me out. I should have posted your letters in a different town.
The Master

The next letter I received from him was still, surprisingly, signed 'The Master'. It was still on a scrappy bit of paper, but now it was abusive, full of aggression and unpleasantness. Subsequent let-ters, following any publication of mine, were equally hostile and still signed 'The Master'. Then one day I received a warm letter and since then there's just been silence. . . .

I won't read you any of the scraps of paper 'The Master' once sent me. Instead I want to introduce you to some marvellous letters – all of them having, incidentally, a tangential medical interest. The first is an ironic comical one by Freud to his disciple Ferenczi, in which he warns him not to kiss his patients.

Sigmund Freud's Letter to Sandor Ferenczi
Written on December 13, 1931

I see that the differences between us come to a head in a technical detail which is well worth discussing. You have not made a secret of the fact that you kiss your patients and let them kiss you; I had also heard that from a patient of my own. Now when you decide to give a full account of your technique and its results you will have to choose between two ways: either you relate this or you conceal it. The latter, as you may well think, is dishonourable. What one does in one's technique one has to defend openly. Besides, both ways soon come together. Even if you don't say so yourself it will soon get known just as I knew it before you told me.

Now I am assuredly not one of those who from prudishness or from consideration of bourgeois convention would condemn little erotic gratifications of this kind. And I am also aware that in the time of the Nibelungs a kiss was a harmless greeting granted to every guest. I am further of the opinion that analysis is possible even in Soviet Russia where so far as the State is concerned there is full sexual freedom. But that does not alter the facts that we are not living in Russia and that with us a kiss signifies a certain erotic intimacy. We have hitherto in our technique held to the conclusion that patients are to be refused erotic gratifications. You know too that where more extensive gratifications are not to be had milder caresses very easily take over their role, in love affairs, on the stage, etc.

Now picture what will be the result of publishing your technique. There is no revolutionary who is not driven out of the field by a still more radical one. A number of independent thinkers in matters of technique will say to themselves: why stop at a kiss? Certainly one gets further when one adopts 'pawing' as well, which after all doesn't make a baby. And then bolder ones will come along who will go further to peeping and showing – and soon we shall have accepted in the technique of analysis the whole repertoire of demiviergerie and petting-parties, resulting in an enormous increase of patients in psycho-analysis among both analysts and patients. The new adherent, however, will easily claim too much of this interest for himself, the younger of our colleagues will find it hard to stop at the point they originally intended, and God the Father, Ferenczi, gazing at the lively scene he has created will perhaps say to himself: maybe after all I should have halted in my technique of motherly affection *before* the kiss. . . .

And the next letter I've chosen is by Dylan Thomas, in which he apologizes for not turning up to a British Medical Association dinner in his home town.

From 'Selected Letters'
DYLAN THOMAS

I plead that the collected will of the Members of the Swansea Branch of the British Medical Association, working by a clinically white magic known only to their profession, drove me, soon after my inexcusable non-appearance at their Annual Dinner, into a bag of sickness and a cropper of accidents from which I have not yet full recovered. The first effect of this malevolent mass medical bedevilment I experienced a week after the Dinner when stopping, heavily disguised, at Swansea in order to learn how really execrated I was in the surgeries and theatres, the bolus-rooms and Celtic lazarets of a town I can approach now only in the deepest dark and where certain areas, particularly around the hospital, are forever taboo to me. I felt sudden and excruciating pains, and when I whimpered about them to a friend he said, 'Whatever you do, don't get ill in Swansea, it's more than your life is worth. Go in with a cough and they'll circumcise you.' So I knew what the position was and I took my pains home. But even at home, word of my unworthiness had reached the doctor's ears, and I was treated like a leper (fortunately, a wrong diagnosis). Ever since then I have felt unwell. A little later I had an attack of gout – undoubtedly the result of some Swansea specialist sticking a pin into a wax toe – and a little later still was set upon by invisible opponents in the bogled Laugharne dark and fell down and cracked my ribs.

Readers: Siân Phillips, David Brierley

Full Selection:
Le Médecin Malgré Lui, MOLIÈRE
A Dangerous Remedy, RHYS DAVIES
Every Day in Every Way, KIT WRIGHT
Hope Against Hope, NADEZHDA MANDELSTAM
A Prince from Western Libya, C. P. CAVAFY
The Cabinet of Pictures, ALLAN CUNNINGHAM
Letter to Sandor Ferenczi Written on December 13, 1931,
    SIGMUND FREUD
A Letter, LUDWIG VAN BEETHOVEN
'Selected Letters', DYLAN THOMAS
Poem in October, DYLAN THOMAS
After a Journey, THOMAS HARDY
The River Merchant's Wife: A Letter, EZRA POUND
Part of Plenty, BERNARD SPENCER
James Joyce's Hundredth Birthday: Side and Front Views, RICHARD
    ELLMANN
Please, MICHAEL BURN

RICHARD ADAMS

1987

*'With Great Pleasure' makes some strange connections. When in 1980
Kingsley Amis recorded his edition he included Philip Larkin's 'Going,
Going', and said: 'He wrote it on a commission from the Department of the Environment, if you can believe such a thing.' Over drinks
after his recording Richard Adams let slip that he was the chap in the
department who had commissioned the poem. For the record, the author*

of Watership Down *knows all the jokes of the 'you've read the book, you've seen the film, now eat the pie' variety.*

I was lucky to have a very happy childhood, and on top of everything else there is one particular respect in which I owe my parents a great debt. They read to me; without compulsion and purely for pleasure; but good stuff and plenty of it. As it seems in memory, neither my father nor my mother was ever too busy for this delightful form of companionship, and each of them appeared to enjoy it every bit as much as I did. While I was quite small – no more than three or four – it was usually my mother who read; before bedtime, as I sat on her knee by the poppling gas fire – I can hear it now – to look at the pictures and ask questions. In this way I made the acquaintance of Peter Rabbit, Pigling Bland and the other Beatrix Potter characters: the Jumblies, the Dong and the other denizens of Edward Lear's world, as depicted so splendidly by Leslie Brooke; together with a host of others less remembered today, such as Bobbity Flop (he was a rabbit, by the way, so I suppose he must have taken root quite deeply), Tony O'Dreams and Little Black Sambo. (No one could see anything the matter with him in those days.) Winnie the Pooh hadn't yet been written.

There was plenty of poetry in this bedtime fare, including Robert Louis Stevenson's *Child's Garden of Verses*, which I've loved ever since. But here, to begin this programme, is another favourite of my mother and myself, which I dare say a good many other infants have cut their literary teeth on during the last hundred years. It's by Eugene Field, an American who died in 1895 at the too-early age of forty-four.

Wynken, Blynken and Nod
EUGENE FIELD

Wynken, Blynken, and Nod one night
Sailed off in a wooden shoe –
Sailed on a river of crystal light,
Into a sea of dew.
'Where are you going, and what do you wish?'
The old moon asked the three.

'We have come to fish for the herring fish
That live in this beautiful sea;
Nets of silver and gold have we!'
      Said Wynken,
      Blynken,
      And Nod.

The old moon laughed and sang a song,
As they rocked in the wooden shoe,
And the wind that sped them all night long
Ruffled the waves of dew.
The little stars were the herring fish
That lived in that beautiful sea –
'Now cast your nets wherever you wish –
Never afeard are we';
So cried the stars to the fishermen three:
      Wynken,
      Blynken,
      And Nod.

All night long their nets they threw
To the stars in the twinkling foam –
Then down from the skies came the wooden shoe,
Bringing the fishermen home;
'Twas all so pretty a sail it seemed
As if it could not be,
And some folks thought 'twas a dream they'd dreamed
Of sailing that beautiful sea –
But I shall name you the fishermen three:
      Wynken,
      Blynken,
      And Nod.

Wynken and Blynken are two little eyes,
And Nod is a little head,
And the wooden shoe that sailed the skies
Is the wee one's trundle-bed.
So shut your eyes while mother sings
Of wonderful sights that be,
And you shall see the beautiful things

As you rock in the misty sea,
Where the old shoe rocked the fishermen three:
> Wynken,
> Blynken,
> And Nod.

I wasn't quite nine when I went to boarding school, and here, lonely and homesick, I came, almost by accident, under the influence of two twentieth-century poets. I suppose many people might think at least one of these, Thomas Hardy, a rather depressing sort of poet for a little boy. However our form-master can't have thought so, because the very first poem I was ever required to learn by heart was Hardy's *When I Set Out for Lyonnesse*. Heaven only knows what the form-master thought it meant. I don't think he could possibly have known that it is Hardy's cryptic and deeply personal account of how, as a young architect in 1870, he travelled, on a winter's day, from Dorset to a North Cornwall vicarage on business, and there met and fell in love with Emma Gifford, the girl he was to marry. I wasn't to know that either, of course: yet the odd truth is that one doesn't need to. What I did grasp clearly and arrestingly was that the poet had made a lonely journey, begun in cold and darkness, to a strange and distant place whence he had returned with the gain of some magical, spiritual blessing. That was quite enough to strike home, whereas the mundane facts would have meant little to a nine-year-old.

When I Set Out for Lyonnesse
THOMAS HARDY

When I set out for Lyonnesse
A hundred miles away,
The rime was on the spray,
And starlight lit my lonesomeness
When I set out for Lyonnesse
A hundred miles away.

What would bechance at Lyonnesse
While I should sojourn there
No prophet durst declare,

Nor did the wisest wizard guess
What would bechance at Lyonnesse
While I should sojourn there.

When I came back from Lyonnesse
With magic in my eyes,
All marked with mute surmise
My radiance rare and fathomless,
When I came back from Lyonnesse
With magic in my eyes!

The other poet was Walter de la Mare, whom later, when I was up at Oxford, I was more than glad to have the chance to meet and thank for all that his work had meant to me. Although de la Mare wrote a great deal of poetry which is ostensibly for children, he is none the less a disturbing poet, inasmuch as his work is shot through and through with a deep awareness of mankind's essential ignorance and insecurity. Life is a prelude to death, and of death we know nothing. In his world cold, ghosts, grief, pain and loss stand all about the little cocooon of bright warmth, which is everywhere pierced by a wild, numinous beauty, often the catalyst of tears and terror rather than delight. He is certainly no orthodox Christian. Yet as a child I was both fascinated and curiously comforted by de la Mare's multifoliate insistence that there exists some strange world beyond our own; a beautiful, if wild and frightening place, with which we have intermittent, tenuous and mysterious contact. Many years later, this idea was to emerge as one of the mainsprings of *Watership Down* – Fiver's gift of second sight – but also as the whole basis of *The Girl in a Swing*. Here is de la Mare at his most grief-stricken and disquieting.

The Ghost
WALTER DE LA MARE

'Who knocks?'/'I, who was beautiful,
Beyond all dreams to restore,
I, from the roots of the dark thorn am hither.
And knock on the door.'

'Who speaks?'/'I – once was my speech
Sweet as the bird's on the air,

When echo lurks by the waters to heed;
'Tis I speak thee fair.'

'Dark is the hour!'/'Ay and cold.'
'Lone is my house.'/'Ah, but mine?'
'Sight, touch, lips, eyes yearned in vain.'
'Long dead these to thine . . .'

Silence. Still faint on the porch
Brake the flames of the stars.
In gloom groped a hope-wearied hand.
Over keys, bolts, and bars.

A face peered. All the grey night
In chaos of vacancy shone;
Nought but vast sorrow was there –
The sweet cheat gone.

At quite an early age, therefore, I had discovered – even though I couldn't have expressed it in words – that while true poetry, like life itself, is often transcendentally beautiful – indeed that is its nature and function – it is also frightening in its manifold reminders that we are not only mortal but ignorant of any ultimate truth. I don't mean that all poetry that is not frightening in this way is of no value. I would express my feeling, I think, in converse terms. Of course there is much true poetry that is not explicitly concerned with our mortality and ignorance – Shakespeare's sonnets, to look no further – but nevertheless any writing, verse or prose, which contrives to ignore or to suggest that we are anything else than mortal and insecure, is shallow and, in effect, mendacious.

By the age of fifteen I was wide open to capture by the sheer *sound* of poetry – the beauty of words and rhythms virtually for their own sake. I was a sitting duck, in fact, for Gerard Manley Hopkins, for T. S. Eliot and even for Edith Sitwell, whom I still admire up to a point. For me the meanings expressed by these poets were secondary to the glorious sound and rhythms of their words. At that time Hopkins' poetry had been in print for only sixteen or seventeen years, and had made an enormous impact on the whole poetic climate of the twenties and thirties. Here is one of his best poems – his elegiac sonnet on the death of one of his parishioners, the village blacksmith, Felix Randal. Incidentally, this was a favourite of George Orwell, who knew it by heart and used to say it over to himself while on night sentry duty during the Spanish Civil War.

Felix Randal
GERARD MANLEY HOPKINS

Felix Randal the farrier, O is he dead then? my duty all ended,
Who have watched his mould of man, big boned and
    hardy-handsome
Pining, pining, till time when reason rambled in it and some
Fatal four disorders, fleshed there, all contended?

Sickness broke him. Impatient, he cursed at first, but mended
Being anointed and all; though a heavenlier heart began some
Months earlier, since I had our sweet reprieve and ransom
Tendered to him. Ah well, God rest him all road ever he
    offended!

This seeing the sick endear them to us, us too it endears.
My tongue had taught thee comfort, touch had quenched thy
    tears,
Thy tears that touched my heart, child, Felix, poor Felix Randal;

How far from then forethought of, all thy more boisterous
    years,
When thou at the random grim forge, powerful amidst peers,
Didst fettle for the great grey drayhorse his bright and battering
    sandal!

Shakespeare, of course, is not really a human being at all. He is like a great mountain upon whose lower slopes we all live, including those who are not consciously aware of it. The mountain affects the weather and the climate. It is a landmark for those far out to sea. We drink from the streams that flow from its heights and pasture our flocks on its slopes. Some people have actually climbed quite a long way up it. I needn't strain the analogy any further; but I will say, loud and clear, that I am in no doubt that by far the greatest secular blessing that we in this country possess in common is that Shakespeare was an Englishman and wrote in English.

Here is Edgar's famous speech from *King Lear*. Edgar, his identity disguised, is setting out to convince his poor old father, the Earl of Gloucester, who has been blinded by his cruel enemies, that the two of them are in fact standing on the summit of Dover cliff. Right at the start, in a miraculous piece of onomatopoeia, Shakespeare sends the vowels hurtling down the cliff from top to bottom. Then the eye follows them.

King Lear
WILLIAM SHAKESPEARE

Come on, sir; here's the place: stand still. How fearful
And dizzy't is to cast one's eye so low!
The crows and choughs that wing the midway air
Show scarce so gross as beetles; half way down
Hangs one that gathers samphire, dreadful trade!
Methinks he seems no bigger than his head.
The fishermen that walk upon the beach
Appear like mice, and yond tall anchoring bark
Diminish'd to her cock, her cock a buoy
Almost too small for sight. The murmuring surge
That on the unnumber'd idle pebbles chafes,
Cannot be heard so high. I'll look no more,
Lest my brain turn, and the deficient sight
Topple down headlong.

Readers: Ronald Pickup, Cheri Lunghi

Full Selection:
Wynken, Blynken and Nod, EUGENE FIELD
When I Set Out for Lyonnesse, THOMAS HARDY
Friends Beyond, THOMAS HARDY
The Ghost, WALTER DE LA MARE
Dream Song, WALTER DE LA MARE
Felix Randal, GERARD MANLEY HOPKINS
The Shield of Achilles, W. H. AUDEN
Oliver Twist, CHARLES DICKENS
Mansfield Park, JANE AUSTEN
King Lear, WILLIAM SHAKESPEARE
Antony and Cleopatra, WILLIAM SHAKESPEARE

BERYL BAINBRIDGE

1981

This fine novelist has recently shown herself to be an accomplished presenter, both on television and on Radio 4's 'Down Your Way'. The personality that comes across in those broadcasts is sympathetic, down to earth, curious, celebratory. Yet, she confessed in her 'With Great Pleasure' programme that she has 'a morbid taste in literature', perhaps because her father wept during the 'sad bits' whilst he read to her when she was a child. Indeed, he made a point of selecting the saddest and gloomiest passages from Dickens. If that was the influence, then it was certainly a powerful one: her selection is characterized by an ineffable tug of sadness.

There was a market in Southport which used to have a stall of second-hand books – I don't know whether it's still there now, probably it is. But as a child I bought several books every week. I didn't always read them, but I liked owning them. One of them was *The Sorrows of Satan* by a woman called Marie Corelli. She was a remarkable writer and a remarkable woman. She used to punt up and down the river at Stratford-on-Avon in a Venetian gondola. In her lifetime she was totally disliked by the press. She was called vain and silly because she swore she was ten years younger than she actually was. But, you see, there was a very sad reason for this – which was only discovered a few years ago. She was illegitimate and her father married her mother when she was eleven years old.

If the critics made fun of her, the public adored her. This particular novel sold 100,000 copies on the first morning of publication. It has a tremendous plot: it's about the devil coming down to live on earth. In this passage Geoffrey, the hero, has discovered that his wife is no better than she ought to be. By this, Geoffrey means that she's taking an unhealthy interest in sex. She's too fond of reading naughty novels.

The Sorrows of Satan
MARIE CORELLI

I found Sybil in the garden, reclining in a basket-chair, her eyes fixed on the after-glow of the sunset, and in her hands a book – one of the loathliest of the prurient novels that have been lately written by women to degrade and shame their sex. With a sudden impulse of rage upon me which I could not resist, I snatched the volume from her and flung it into the lake below. She made no movement of either surprise or offence – she merely turned her eyes away from the glowing heavens, and looked at me with a little smile.

'The new fiction is detestable,' – I said hotly – 'Both in style and morality. Even as a question of literature I wonder at your condescending to read any of it. The woman whose dirty book I have just thrown away – and I feel no compunction for having done it – is destitute of grammar as well as decency.'

'Oh, but the critics don't notice that,' – she interrupted, with a delicate mockery vibrating in her voice – 'It is apparently not their business to assist in preserving the purity of the English language. What they fall into raptures over is the originality of the "sexual" theme, though I should have thought all such matters were as old as the hills. I never read reviews as a rule, but I did happen to come across one on the book you have just drowned – and in it the reviewer stated he had cried over it!'

She laughed again. My God.

What was the use of living on. Knowing that she whom I had loved, and whom I loved still in a way that was hateful to myself, was a thing viler and more shameless in character than the veriest poor drab of the street who sells herself for current coin – that the lovely body and angel-face were but an attractive disguise for the soul of a harpy – a vulture of vice, . . .

My thoughts went on and on in the never-ending circle and problem of incurable, unspeakable despair.

16

I went for two years to a boarding school in Hertfordshire. And at half-term my parents came up to London and stayed at the Regent Palace Hotel. I used to meet them in the tea room there. And I remember the palm trees and the orchestra, and the splendid occasion when my father punched a man on the nose because he winked at my mother. My father called him a 'lounge lizard'.

Ever since then I've been fascinated by hotels, and I particularly like this poem by John Betjeman.

The Flight from Bootle
JOHN BETJEMAN

Lonely in the Regent Palace,
    Sipping her 'Banana Blush',
Lilian lost sight of Alice
    In the honey-coloured rush.

Settled down at last from Bootle,
    Alice whispered, 'Just a min,
While I pop upstairs and rootle
    For another safety pin.'

Dreamy from the band pavilion
    Drops of the *Immortal Hour*
Fell around the lonely Lilian
    Like an ineffectual shower.

Half an hour she sat and waited
    In the honey-coloured lounge,
Till she with herself debated,
    'Time for me to go and scrounge!'

Time enough! or not enough time!
    Lilian, you wait in vain;
Alice will not have a rough time,
    Nor be quite the same again.

We used to go over the holiday to the Herbert Arms Hotel, which was in Chirbury in Shropshire. With a bit of a stretch of the imagination you could call it a coaching inn. Next door to the hotel lived a man who fell in love with a land-girl. I wish I could

say her name was Miranda, but it wasn't. Every night the man
next door would lean out of his window waiting for the girl. In the
bar downstairs in the Inn, people sang and stamped their feet.
The girl jilted the man, and one night he took a shot gun and
stalked the graveyard in the moonlight. He didn't shoot anybody, but when I first heard 'Tarantella' by Hilaire Belloc, it
reminded me of him.

Tarantella
HILAIRE BELLOC

Do you remember an Inn,
Miranda?
Do you remember an Inn?
And the tedding and the spreading
Of the straw for a bedding,
And the fleas that tease in the High Pyrenees,
And the wine that tasted of the tar?
And the cheers and the jeers of the young muleteers
(Under the vine of the dark verandah)?
Do you remember an Inn, Miranda,
Do you remember an Inn?
And the cheers and the jeers of the young muleteers
Who hadn't got a penny,
And who weren't paying any,
And the hammer at the doors and the Din?
And the Hip! Hop! Hap!
Of the clap
Of the hands to the twirl and the swirl
Of the girl gone chancing,
Glancing
Dancing,
Backing and advancing,
Snapping of a clapper to the spin
Out and in –
And the Ting, Tong, Tang of the guitar!
Do you remember an Inn,
Miranda?
Do you remember an Inn!

Never more;
Miranda,
Never more.
Only the high peaks hoar:
And Aragon a torrent at the door.
No sound
In the walls of the Halls where falls
The tread
Of the feet of the dead to the ground
No sound:
But the boom
Of the far Waterfall like Doom.

When I was a child, Shirley Temple appeared in a film called *The Bluebird*, based on a book by Maeterlinck – there wasn't a dry eye in the cinema. And not long afterwards – again in Southport, at the bookstall – I bought for tuppence something by Maeterlinck called *The Life of the Bee*. When I first read it I thought it had something to do with religion. I still read it. I think it's both sinister and awe-inspiring.

The Life of the Bee
MAETERLINCK

Our hive, then, is preparing to swarm; making ready for the great immolation to the exacting gods of the race. In obedience to the order of the spirit – an order that to us may well seem incomprehensible, for it is utterly opposed to all our own instincts and feelings – 60 or 70,000 bees out of the 80 or 90,000 that form the whole population, will abandon the maternal city at the prescribed hour. They will not leave at a moment of despair; or desert with sudden and wild resolve, a home laid waste by famine, disease or war.

No: the exile has long been planned, and the favourable hour patiently waited. Were the hive poor, had it suffered from pillage or storm, had misfortune befallen the royal family, the bees would not forsake it. They leave it only when it has attained the apogee of its prosperity; at a time when, after the arduous labours

19

of the spring, the immense palace of wax has its 120,000 well-arranged cells overflowing with new honey, and with the many-coloured flour, known as 'bees' bread', on which nymphs and larvae are fed.

Never is the hive more beautiful than on the eve of its heroic renouncement, in its unrivalled hour of fullest abundance and joy; serene, for all its apparent excitement and feverishness. Let us endeavour to picture it to ourselves – not as it appears to the bees, for we cannot tell in what magical, formidable fashion things may be reflected in the 6 or 7,000 facets of their lateral eyes and the triple cyclopean eye on their brow – but as it would seem to us, were we of their stature. From the height of a dome more colossal than that of St Peter's at Rome, waxen walls descend to the ground, balanced in the void and the darkness; gigantic and manifold, vertical and parallel geometric constructions, to which, for relative precision, audacity, and vastness, no human structure is comparable.

Each of these walls, whose substance still is immaculate and fragrant, of virginal, silvery freshness, contains thousands of cells stored with provisions sufficient to feed the whole population for several weeks. Here, lodged in transparent cells, are the pollens, love-ferment of every flower of spring, making brilliant splashes of red and yellow, of black and mauve.

Close by, sealed with a seal to be broken only in days of supreme distress, the honey of April is stored, most limpid and perfumed of all, in 20,000 reservoirs that form a long and magnificent embroidery of gold, whose borders hang stiff and rigid. Still lower the honey of May matures, in great open vats by whose side watchful cohorts maintain an incessant current of air. In the centre, and far from the light whose diamond rays steal in through the only opening, in the warmest part of the hive, there stands the abode of the future; here does it sleep, and wake. For this is the royal domain of the brood-cells, set apart for the queen and her acolytes; about 10,000 cells wherein the eggs repose, 15 or 16,000 chambers tenanted by larvae, 40,000 dwellings inhabited by white nymphs to whom thousands of nurses minister. And finally, in the holy of holies of these parts there are three, four, six or twelve sealed palaces, vast in size compared with the others, where the adolescent princesses lie who await

their hour; wrapped in a kind of shroud, all of them motionless
and pale, and fed in the darkness.

Readers: Alan Dobie, Rosalind Shanks

Full Selection:
Little Gidding, T. S. ELIOT
The Sorrows of Satan, MARIE CORELLI
The Flight from Bootle, JOHN BETJEMAN
The Life of the Bee, MAETERLINCK
Dover Beach, MATTHEW ARNOLD
Therese at the Hotel, FRANÇOIS MAURIAC
Tarantella, HILAIRE BELLOC
At the Villa Madeira, GAVIN EWART
The Body in the Library, AGATHA CHRISTIE
The Big Sleep, RAYMOND CHANDLER
Lolita, VLADIMIR NABOKOV
The Worst Journey in the World, APSLEY CHERRY-GARRARD
Dombey and Son, CHARLES DICKENS

PETER BARKWORTH

1986

*Peter Barkworth is, of course, a gifted actor – one of the few who make the
words 'quality television' not seem like a contradiction in terms – but he is
also a charming man. Once, during a read-through for someone else's
'With Great Pleasure', he was roughly rebuked by the presenter for not
performing a poem in the way that he, the presenter, preferred. Not
having been given any indication that he should read it in a particular*

manner, Peter Barkworth had, correctly, offered an interpretation of his own. He responded to what was little less than an insult with great courtesy, and complied with what was wanted. When, shortly afterwards, I offered him the opportunity to present an edition of his own, I imagined that he would, like most actors, choose to read half the items himself, but not a bit of it. Even his beloved Siegfried Sassoon was left in the admittedly safe hands of Alec McCowen whilst he confined himself to presenting a most entertaining selection.

I think the writer I feel, and have always felt, most at home with is Siegfried Sassoon, maybe because he lived in Kent and loved it as much as I do, maybe because I've always felt specially drawn to the writers of his period – Wilfred Owen, Rupert Brooke, Robert Graves – and maybe because he wrote a lot about his childhood; and I first read his books when I was a schoolboy.

In this poem, 'Doggerel About Old Days', which he wrote in 1939, he looks back to when he was a young man of twenty-three, living a happy and comparatively carefree life, before the onslaught of the First World War.

Doggerel About Old Days
SIEGFRIED SASSOON

Young people now – they don't know what the past was like.
Then one could find the main roads museful on one's bike.
Give *me* a moment and I'm back in Kent; I know
How safe and sound life struck me thirty years ago.

Passenger trains puffed on through landscapes then like Time;
And this year with its next year found an easy rhyme.
Uninterrupted cricket seasons were to come.
Beanfields were good to smell and bees would always hum
In trees that knew no threat of overhead invasion.
One liked the foreground future, needing no persuasion.

Kent was all sleepy villages through which I went
Carrying my cricket bag. In wintertime, content
To follow hounds across wet fields, I jogged home tired.
In 1909 the future was a thing desired.

22

I travelled on; the train was Time; Kent was the scene;
And where I was I felt that, as I'd always been,
I should continue unperturbed in storm and shine.
Will someone tell me where I am – in '39?

When I became a RADA student in 1946, we all had to learn at least two pieces a week for diction and voice production classes. We boomed out loads of Auden, Eliot and Dylan Thomas, who were all the rage then, so it was always a relief when someone found something different, like a girl did one day, surprising us all with this new poem by the newly-discovered Dorothy Parker.

Symptom Recital
DOROTHY PARKER

I do not like my state of mind;
I'm bitter, querulous, unkind.
I hate my legs, I hate my hands,
I do not yearn for lovelier lands.
I dread the dawn's recurrent light;
I hate to go to bed at night.
I snoot at simple, earnest folk.
I cannot take the gentlest joke.
I find no peace in paint or type.
My world is but a lot of tripe.
I'm disillusioned, empty-breasted.
For what I think, I'd be arrested.
I am not sick. I am not well.
My quondam dreams are shot to hell.
My soul is crushed, my spirit sore;
I do not like me any more.
I cavil, quarrel, grumble, grouse.
I ponder on the narrow house.
I shudder at the thought of men . . .
I'm due to fall in love again.

Of course, all self-respecting drama students knew Hamlet's advice to the players off by heart too. I'm always amazed at how modern it sounds, and what good advice it has remained for actors and actresses over the years.

Hamlet's Advice to the Players
WILLIAM SHAKESPEARE

Speak the speech, I pray you, as I pronounc'd it to you, trippingly on the tongue; but if you mouth it, as many of your players do, I had as lief the town-crier spoke my lines. Nor do not saw the air too much with your hand, thus, but use all gently: for in the very torrent, tempest, and, as I may say, the whirlwind of passion, you must acquire and beget a temperance that may give it smoothness. O! it offends me to the soul to hear a robustious periwig-pated fellow tear a passion to tatters, to very rags, to split the ears of the groundlings, who for the most part are capable of nothing but inexplicable dumb-shows, and noise: I would have such a fellow whipp'd for o'erdoing Termagant; it out-herods Herod: pray you, avoid it.

Be not too tame neither, but let your own discretion be your tutor: suit the action to the word, the word to the action; with this special observance, that you o'erstep not the modesty of nature; for any thing so overdone is from the purpose of playing, whose end, both at the first and now, was and is, to hold, as 'twere, the mirror up to nature; to show virtue her own feature, scorn her own image, and the very age and body of the time his form and pressure. Now, this overdone or come tardy off, though it make the unskilful laugh, cannot but make the judicious grieve; the censure of the which one must in your allowance o'erweigh a whole theatre of others. O! there be players that I have seen play, and heard others praise, and that highly, not to speak it profanely, that, neither having the accent of Christians nor the gait of Christian, pagan, nor man, have so strutted and bellowed that I have thought some of nature's journeymen had made men and not made them well, they imitated humanity so abominably.

O! reform it altogether. And let those that play your clowns speak no more than is set down for them; for there be of them that will themselves laugh, to set on some quantity of barren spectators to laugh too, though in the mean time some necessary question of the play be then to be considered; that's villainous, and shows a most pitiful ambition in the fool that uses it. Go, make you ready.

When we left RADA – I don't know if they do it now – we were all presented with a most curious little black book called *The RADA Graduate's Keepsake and Counsellor* which makes very odd reading nowadays because it's so old-fashioned – not at all like Hamlet's advice. Distinguished actors and actresses contributed to it, and there is this delightful bit about correct behaviour in the theatre from Athene Seyler.

The RADA Graduate's Keepsake and Counsellor
ATHENE SEYLER

I would like to emphasise that it is not good manners to throw cigarette ends on the stage at rehearsals, and leave the floor littered with stamped-out ends. If smoking is allowed by a Producer (which it ought not to be), and no ash trays are provided, the company must dispose of its cigarette stubs outside the theatre. I, personally, deplore the habit of addressing everybody by their Christian names before any personal intimacy has been established; and think that, at rehearsals certainly, the junior members of a company should formally address the others. And, above all, no one should ever try to put the blame for missing an entrance on the Call Boy. Every actor when called, or even when he hears the general call of 'Overture' or the Act beginning, should reply by thanking the Call Boy, to show that he has been heard. If this were universally done, it would be in the nature of signing for a message, and would protect the defenceless Call Boy, who is – in any case – a courtesy provided by the Management and not a right of the Actor.

I don't quite know why I keep a diary, but I do, and have done so every day since January 1968. That's millions and millions of words, it seems. It helps relieve my feelings and gets things off my chest, but it's also nice to have an accurate record of events and opinions. Of course the length of each entry is always determined by how much time I've got to write it, because I always do it the following morning. Sometimes it's just 'Sorry diary, no time today', but at other times it's pages and pages, especially, of course, when I haven't been too happy about things. Hugh Walpole was very good about diaries in his.

25

Hugh Walpole's Diary

19th June 1924. Two rules for every honest diarist: One – no self-consciousness. Two – no sense of shame. Three – no false modesty. Four – no sham bravery. Five – no fine writing. Six – no fear of indecencies. Seven – no scorn of trivialities. Eight – no self disgust. There are others but these will do.

Well, for a start: I am forty years of age, have published seventeen volumes of more or less merit (cf rule 3: no false modesty), I am single and shall always be so, in excellent health save for toothache and neuralgia, never constipated, always sleep well, owe some five hundred pounds, am owed four thousand.

Now as to my character: I am kind-hearted, but have to rouse myself to take trouble. I am very sensual, but pious and pure if that sensuality is gratified. I am very non-condemnatory unless I am attacked, when I at once accuse the attacker of every crime. I am very generous about large sums and inclined to be mean about small ones. I adore to be in love but am bored if someone is much in love with me. I am superficially both conceited and vain but at heart consider myself with a good deal of contempt.

6th January 1926: (Question this!) I am greatly interested in the question of a future life but until it is settled the thought of it influences my conduct but little.

28th October 1932: (It occupies me more and more). I adore beauty in all its forms. I hate to see others suffer. I am a great coward but can be roused to endurance. I have a sense of humour which I get only too little into my work.

I couldn't resist including here a speech from Tom Kempinski's marvellous play *Duet for One*. It's about a concert violinist who contracted multiple sclerosis and therefore couldn't play any more. She talks about it to a psychiatrist, Dr Feldmann, and tells him what music means to her.

Duet for One
TOM KEMPINSKI

Well – music. Music. Music, Dr Feldmann, is the purest expression of humanity that there is. Because, you see, it's magic; but real magic, true mystery, not trickery. You can say it is sound, as speech is sound, as bird-song is sound, but it isn't. It's itself. A piece of music which expresses pain or sorrow, or loneliness, it sounds nothing like what a lonely man says or does, but expresses it, and even better than the person does. Magic. You see, there's no God, you know, Dr Feldmann, but I know where they got the idea; they got it from music. It is a kind of heaven. It's unearthly. It lifts you out of life to another place.

And later, at the end of the play, she says:

Look, Dr Feldmann, I played the violin, because when Mummy died, the real world, your world, the world of jobs, Daddy's world, it disappeared; shattered. So I had to build another world, what you'd call a fantasy world. My new world was filled with the pain and the sorrow and the despair of the loss and the awful unfamiliar changes. So I hung on to the only world I had: music. My violin. And I sang the song of the pain and the sorrow and the loss and the awful changes, to soothe myself. And I sang for dear life – literally for life, 'cos it was all I had. And suddenly the song turned to one of joy, because of the beauty of the music; and I was ecstatic that I had turned such sorrow to happiness, because the change was such a relief, such a wonderful pleasure. And now I can't play any more. And because the shock and the pain were so awful again at this new loss, I tried to pretend I could cross back over to the old world and stupid little plans, like being David's secretary. But I'm not there, Dr Feldmann. The violin isn't my work; it isn't a way of life. It's where I live. It's when I play that I actually live in the real world; mine, of course. So what can you do? What can you possibly do, when I can't cross over? It's not your fault. It's not that you haven't got the skill. It's just that I'm over here – and I can't sing. . . .

Readers: Alec McCowen, Penelope Wilton

Full Seiection:
Doggerel About Old Days, SIEGFRIED SASSOON
Symptom Recital, DOROTHY PARKER
Hamlet's Advice to the Players, WILLIAM SHAKESPEARE
The RADA Graduate's Keepsake and Counsellor, ATHENE SEYLER
A Postillion Struck by Lightning, DIRK BOGARDE
The Waves, VIRGINIA WOOLF
Absence Makes the Heart Grow Heart Trouble, OGDEN NASH
A Love, C. P. CAVAFY
Extract from the Diaries of Hugh Walpole
Full Circle, JANET BAKER
Duet for One, TOM KEMPINSKI
Skimbleshanks – The Railway Cat, T. S. ELIOT

ALAN BLEASDALE

1983

I think it's fair to say that Alan Bleasdale first became known to the public at large when his 'Boys from the Blackstuff' was shown on television. 'Gissa job', the bitter catchphrase uttered by its central character, Yosser Hughes, will linger in the British consciousness long after the circumstances which brought it into being will (hopefully) have become a distant memory. Bleasdale's personality, as it comes across from his 'With Great Pleasure', is one of a shy and sensitive, noisy extrovert. At the age of eighteen, 'full of football, fear, anxiety, Chandler, Brian Rix, Orwell and Heller, Hemingway and Greene, lust and Lenny Bruce', he used to take girls to poetry readings because it didn't cost too much and to show them that the footballing drunkard was also a sensitive soul who 'knew for a fact *that 17th Century Bacon wasn't an old piece of pork'. If the last item seems a little dated now, with Reagan no longer President, and an arms agreement having just been signed, chilling as ever, it still serves as a reminder of a near miss, and a warning.*

The biggest problem I've had with compiling the pieces is the sense of abject disappointment I've had when I've gone back to books and plays that I used to love years ago, that I thought I must still love today. That I can't stand anymore. This programme could very easily have been called *With Great Disinterest.*

Another difficulty I had was trying to break into the most brilliant books and plays and just rob the best bit of them – like stealing the smile off the *Mona Lisa.* 'Hey, hey boys, I got the smile!' And ruined the picture.

I was advised to look for a theme: you know, childhood, birth, marriage, the nobility of pain, the consequence of suffering, the influence of Ian Botham on the contestants for the Nobel Peace Prize. So, I got all the pieces together, and I looked at what I had, *and* . . . I couldn't find one. I mean, I have enough problems finding themes in my own work, never mind anyone else's. The pieces I have chosen are the things that have touched me to tears or to terror, laughter as I've gone along. And perhaps that's a theme in itself.

The book that had the biggest influence on my whole life without any shadow of a doubt is the Catholic Catechism. The Catechism of the Christian Doctrine. It's the most frightening book in the whole world. When you don't know it. When you're seven years old. And when you had a teacher like I had at the start of the Juniors. It's a big year that – yer first confession, yer first Holy communion, yer first inklings of mortality, yer first trip to Chester Zoo – and there's this sarcastic atheist in Catholic clothing stood at the front of the class with the kind of acid wit that would shrivel anything, especially a sensitive, shy, sweet little seven-year-old boy. You see, the first Tuesday in every month, the priest would come in to test us on the Catechism and the Ten Commandments . . . and the first Monday in every month, Dorothy Parker's bitter sister would be there, breathing fire and polo mints, testing us for our test. It went something like this:

29

TEACHER:	Bleasdale.
BLEASDALE:	Yes Miss.
TEACHER:	You first. Do you know why you're first?
BLEASDALE:	No Miss.
TEACHER:	Because you're a congenital idiot, Bleasdale, and if you know the answers, I can be fairly certain that the rest of the class will.
BLEASDALE:	Yes Miss. Thank you Miss.
TEACHER:	Now then, let's see if we can improve on your previous attempt, shall we? I don't think Father McMahon was over enamoured with your religious knowledge on the last occasion, do you, boy?
BLEASDALE:	No Miss.
TEACHER:	I don't think anyone could be too impressed with your rendition of Our Father. Our Father, who art in Heaven, Harold be his name indeed. The Blessed Trinity, Bleasdale.
BLEASDALE:	Er . . . yes Miss?
TEACHER:	Who or what are they?
BLEASDALE:	Er, God the Father.
TEACHER:	Whose name is not Harold.
BLEASDALE:	Er, God the Son . . . God the Father, God the Son and er. . . .
DONOVAN:	(whispers) God the Holy Ghost, Bleasy.
BLEASDALE:	God the Holy Ghost. Miss.
TEACHER:	Very good, Donovan, your lips didn't move once, but don't go Educating Archie, thank you. . . . What are you, Bleasdale, tell me, what are you?
BLEASDALE:	I'm a genital idiot, Miss.
TEACHER:	Well, I suppose there's always a chance you can be run over by a bus before tomorrow's test – the seventh commandment, boy, the one between six and eight.
BLEASDALE:	Thou shalt not . . . er, thou shalt not. . . .
TEACHER:	. . . Thou is not capable of. . . .
BLEASDALE:	Thou shalt not steal?
TEACHER:	No.
BLEASDALE:	Murder?

30

TEACHER: I'm considering it, child.

BLEASDALE: Er, cover thy neighbour's wife, er, in a field, with his ass. On a Sabbath, Miss.

TEACHER: You are doomed, boy, doomed.

BLEASDALE: Thank you, Miss.

TEACHER: What is the seventh commandment, Donovan?

DONOVAN: Thou shalt not commit adultery, Miss.

TEACHER: Very good, Donovan, very good.

DONOVAN: Er, what is adultery, Miss?

TEACHER: We teach you that in the seniors, Donovan. Now then, what's mortal sin?

DONOVAN: Mortal sin is a grievous sin against God, Miss.

TEACHER: Why is it called mortal sin?

DONOVAN: It is called mortal sin because it kills the soul and deserves Hell, Miss.

TEACHER: Is it a great evil to fall into mortal sin?

DONOVAN: It is the greatest of all evils to fall into mortal sin, miss.

TEACHER: Where will they go who die in mortal sin?

DONOVAN: They who die in mortal sin will go to hell for all eternity, Miss.

TEACHER: Good. And how should you finish the day, Donovan?

DONOVAN: I should finish the day by kneeling down and saying my night prayers, Miss.

TEACHER: And after your night prayers what should you do?

DONOVAN: After my night prayers I should observe due modesty in going to bed, and then occupy myself with thoughts of death. Miss.

'Occupy myself with thoughts of death.' I did that alright. I was terrified out of my tiny mind, not least of all when one particular first Tuesday in the month, the regular priest failed to sober up in time, and Canon O'Reilly arrived at the classroom door. To be greeted with the same joyful rapture that the City of London greeted the Great Plague of 1665.

My unabiding memory is of this unshaven hulk with a nose the colour of Lent, standing wild-eyed above me, smelling of incense and cigarettes, as I stared at the buttons of his fly and completely failed even to begin *The Apostles' Creed*. And then he bent down, squashing to death the two kids directly in front of me, and thirty years of Christian wisdom hurtled from deep within him: 'You boy, you, of one thing be certain; when you die, when you die you will go to eternal Hell!'

I had a nervous breakdown during playtime. I mean, what kind of a future could you believe in, if you were deprived of the consolation of Heaven when you kicked it? – when all it came down to at the end of the day, when the plugs were pulled, was standing there between Adolf Hitler and Attila the Hun, stoking coal, with forked ears, two lungfuls of soot, a tail between your legs, and Beelzebub as your foreman. On twenty-four-hour nights.

And to be quite honest, I still carry the scars of my Catholic education, the catechism and the commandments, and the way they were taught – death threats at seven – even now, more than thirty years later.

I first met Willy Russell in 1974, when I was in my late twenties and he, as he occasionally delights in reminding me, was somewhat younger. I'd just written this first novel that was about to be published, that I confidently expected to attract the attention of the Booker Prize Committee, and he was in the middle of struggling with a mere trifle, a little piece for the Everyman Theatre called *John, Paul, George, Ringo and Bert*.

In Liverpool I'm always asked how we get on with each other, and I can only reply that we're best friends and mortal enemies – somewhat similar to Liverpool and Everton footballers, who twice a year spend ninety minutes kicking lumps out of each other, and then go and get legless together all over the clubs in town.

Anyway, I give him my plays to read hot off the typewriter, and he gives me his. I knew, for example, that *Educating Rita* was going to be a smash hit, a huge success, that it would run and run, and run, and the prospect sickened me for weeks.

But it's alright. No, it is. Because while Willy spends half his time being congratulated on writing *Boys from the Blackstuff*, *The Muscle Market* and *Having a Ball*, I regularly have drinks bought for me because I wrote *Educating Rita*, *The Daughters of Albion* and *Our*

32

Day Out. I kid you not. To the point that last summer as I walked towards the Liverpool Playhouse, two girls went past me, and one said to the other, 'That's the feller what wrote Educating Willy.'

What I really think about Willy Russell is that at his finest no one else depicts better, or more comically and truthfully, humanity's inner emptiness, despair and desire for escape. In *One for the Road*, Dennis, on the edge of his thirtieth birthday and a complete crack-up, is being treated by his wife Pauline to a birthday dinner in their new house on a new estate full of the new middle classes. Dennis's mother and father are late. Pauline goes to answer the 'phone.

One for the Road
WILLY RUSSELL

If that's your mother, I'll answer it. . . . Mother, you were supposed to be coming early. . . . But I told you to get off at the first bus stop. . . . Dennis, they've got lost! They got off at the wrong bus stop again. . . . Mother, you've been to the bungalow God knows how many times. Why can't you or Dad remember where it is? . . . Oh no, they don't all look alike. . . . We do not have a number because we do not like to deface the facade of the bungalow. . . . Look, exactly where are you? . . . Right. Now listen, go out of William Tell Avenue, take the first right into Wagner Walk. Go along Wagner Walk, up Elgar Drive into Beethoven Close and you'll see Brahms Close. Go down there, turn into Mahler Crescent and we're three down from 'Rivendell'. . . . No, no number, just 'The Haven'. . . .

Like absolutely everyone, to a larger or lesser degree, I'm the normal confusions. Moralist and thief, generous and mean, an anarchist most likely to break the legs of anyone trying to take my property, an atheist most happy to pray at the least opportunity or need. And, of course, I hate violence. So much so that when I see it, I usually join in. Naturally, like any *Guardian* reader, I also find the thought of taking life the deepest of all offences and, consequently, capital punishment a horror in itself. And yet . . . and yet, there is a part of me that is still swinging and grunting from tree to tree.

About eighteen months ago, we five Bleasdales and those five Russells spent a weekend on a camp site in Anglesea. On the Saturday night we all went for a drink in this pub on the coast, the kind that cater for children – you know, they lock them in a secure room with a security guard on the door – no, there was a games room, an animal den and a sweet counter between the games room and the lounge. To cut a long story short, I was playing snooker with our eldest, my wife was with the youngest, and our daughter, the middle child, was with my wife. Well, that is, I thought she was with my wife . . . while my wife thought she was with me. And she had been with both of us, but not for over twenty minutes, when she'd gone to queue at the sweet counter.

The place was packed to bursting point. And I burst through it, more and more panic as the moments went by, and Willy and Ann and my wife, Julie, with that feeling that only parents can possibly describe, they too ran from room to room . . . and I ran into the road, through the car park and down to the beach . . . and then started running after cars as they left the pub. . . .

And I tell you now, if anyone had taken our daughter away and I had found him there and then that night, I would have killed him. I would have, as they say, torn him limb from limb. . . . Our daughter was found crying, still queueing at the very front of the sweet counter, well hidden and very squashed by the other bigger kids around her.

A week later I read an article by Philip Norman in the *Sunday Times*, and I wrote my first letter to a journalist. Because I recognized that horrifying feeling of total helplessness and rage that he wrote about.

He wrote in response to a tide of murder, to the Beiruts and Belfasts and the brutal batterings that barely make a paragraph now in even our local newspapers. He wrote in memory of growing up in the fifties, in what he calls 'the great hush that seemed to enfold the world' – and to the fact that in separate incidents two people very close to him had been attacked by an intruder and might have been killed.

Some of you, sitting comfortably, some distance from Anglesea, may disagree passionately with his conclusions, but by God I recognize the *feelings*.

34

On a Tide of Murder
PHILIP NORMAN

Like most children, I was afraid of the dark. I imagined, lying in bed, that 'murderers' were coming up the stairs. In time, I was comforted to realise my own insignificance. Who would want to be bothered to murder me? Murderers, I saw thankfully, belonged to a distant, highly idiosyncratic class, like Christie, or Ruth Ellis, the 'Mews Murderess' whose execution took place just before our school Assembly. I know because a boy came up to me, looked at his watch and said, 'Well, that's the end of Ruth Ellis.' Obscurely but powerfully, I felt the night was safe again.

But now I know that it is my destiny, and yours, to live in a world grown infinitely more terrifying than childhood's worst nightmares. I know that, on the contrary, almost anybody can be bothered to murder me.

We speak of civilisations that 'toppled', of the 'fall' of Athens or Rome, of a 'Dark Age' dropped over Europe like a sack. We choose not to recognise that, wherever chaos and terror have triumphed, it was slowly, through the bewildered acquiescence of millions of people like ourselves. They too tried not to worry; to get on with life. They moved, as we are moving, unconsciously with the tide of murder, from disbelieving horror to dazed unshockability.

The special paradox of our Dark Age is that it should have grown in the tatters of an era when 'peace' and 'love' were words in serious widespread use. Today's urban terrorist wears the blue jeans and amulets of yesterday's smiling liberal. The Maze 'hunger strikers', those empty, almost ectoplasmic faces, wear their hair long the way young men did as a plea for tolerance and a declaration of non-violence. The contagion took root, not in Dallas in 1963 but in California in 1969. We are menaced not by the children of Marx, but of Manson.

Our blindness is increased by our gigantic power of sight, through television: by habituation to terrible sights and, equally, by the growing adeptness of those responsible in hiding their crimes within language of perverted blandness. It strikes no one as strange any more when three madmen, machine-gunning an airport lounge, call themselves a 'popular front', when a hostage is butchered by a 'people's court'; when those who use children to plant explosives term themselves 'freedom fighters'; when innocent shopping crowds are 'targets'; or when the Provisional IRA, after ambushing a milk float, claim 'responsibility'.

In the age of the bloody mind, I can feel my own mind growing as bloody as the next. When I read that a bomb-maker has blown himself up, I feel quiet satisfaction at Fate's occasional symmetry. And I have come to believe in the death penalty, as a deterrent to those many crimes based on pure cowardice, and to eradicate – as has been justly done before – self-evident, unmitigated evil. I remember the words of Dr Herrema, the Dutchman whose intellectual toughness all but mesmerised his Irish kidnappers. 'Don't you realise?' he asked them at one point. 'These conditions are worse than in Belsen.'

As a child, my biggest nightmare contained men wearing hoods, with holes out for their eyes and mouths. The Fifties melted them at dawn, into sun and sticky buds. The Eighties legitimise them, slow-marching in Ulster. They are death embodied – perhaps yours, perhaps mine. I myself fear death as much as in childhood. But I see now what people throughout history must have seen in their own terror times: that death can be something you choose. It is preferable to the suffering of my family, or to life in any world where the hooded ones hold power.

Here to end are the words of Ronald Reagan, at a press conference without his auto-cue, without anyone to translate into any kind of intelligent language, in other words, without help except himself. The question asked was: 'Could Battlefield nuclear weapons be fired without the inevitable consequence of an intercontinental nuclear exchange between the Super Powers?'

President Reagan at a Press Conference

Well, I would – if they realised that we, again – if we led them back to that stalemate only because that our retaliatory power, our seconds, or our strike at them after their first strike at us would be so destructive that they couldn't afford it. That would hold them off. . . . Yes.

Readers: Julie Walters, Michael Angelis

Full Selection:
Catechism and Ten Commandments, ALAN BLEASDALE
Sad Aunt Marge, ROGER McGOUGH
Little Johnny's Confession, BRIAN PATTEN
Love from Arthur Rainbow, ADRIAN HENRI
One for the Road, WILLY RUSSELL
Educating Rita, WILLY RUSSELL
Flying Blind, BILL MORRISON
Lost and Found Advertisement, PRIVATE EYE
Hollywood Quotes
On a Tide of Murder, PHILIP NORMAN
Quotation, LENNY BRUCE
Press Conference, PRESIDENT REAGAN

HEATHER COUPER

1987

'Are you astronomy or media?' It was, I imagine, a not uncommon greeting between two strangers brought together at any gathering organized by Heather Couper and her partner Nigel Henbest. They have formed a company, 'Hencoup', with the express purpose of bringing a greater knowledge of astronomy to the world at large – no doubt they would argue to the world at small. As someone who has a tolerable acquaintance with black holes, but could positively identify a great bear only in a zoo, I find their conversation stimulating and enlightening. Heather endeared herself to me when she arrived for the rehearsal of her programme, recorded appropriately enough in the old Royal Observatory at Greenwich, and announced that she had just bought a copy of volume 1

of this anthology. 'Naturally,' I said, 'I shall be including you in volume 2.' 'Oh good,' she said. 'I mean, oh dear. What will you say about me?' At this point I ought to mention the subsidiary activity of their company, the fermenting of a wine known as 'Château Hencoup'. It is very . . . distinctive. Indeed I would have argued that it spoilt you for anything else, but at a subsequent meeting in a Covent Garden wine bar I was relieved to see everyone present managing a bucket or two of house white. 'Media,' I said, but by the end of the evening I am not at all sure that I would have known the answer to the question.

Via a year working as a dogsbody at the Cambridge observatories I went off to the University of Leicester and started studying for a degree in astro-physics. Now, when one is at university one tends to take up other interests as well as one's subject and one of my really all-pervading interests changed from astronomy to gastronomy, which I'm still fascinated by. Perhaps that's one of the reasons why I live in Greenwich where there are so many good restaurants and wine bars! As well as an interest in gastronomy I did become interested in other food for thought, I should say, theatre, music and painting. I did become interested in music of a very early period, the sixteenth, seventeenth and eighteenth centuries. What I like particularly about Baroque music and indeed earlier Renaissance music is how people could get away with such completely undiluted emotion. You could wallow on about your inconstant love affairs until you were blue in the face and everybody thought it was fabulous: odes to this, that and the other and terrible things that would happen to your heart, you could cry about them to your heart's content.

I was equally drawn to the poetry of the time and for me nobody can sum up the poetry of the Renaissance era so beautifully as John Donne. As well as the angst of inconstancy to be found in such poems as 'Now That Thou Hast Lov'd Me One Whole Day' Donne also found permanence, some of his poems are extremely beautiful and they do talk about true love. I like in one poem in particular about permanence how he weaves in contemporary observations of what else was going on in the world that surrounded him, by which I mean the voyages of exploration, new techniques in map-making, explorations of new cities, even new financial means of dealing with merchants and so on. In the following poem you will see there are references towards the end of the work of the mappers by which he means the work of the astronomers. I love this poem very very deeply because it means a great deal to me and my own feelings on permanence.

The Good Morrow
JOHN DONNE

I wonder by my troth, what thou, and I
   Did, till we loved? were we not weaned till then,
But sucked on country pleasures, childishly?
   Or snorted we in the seven sleepers' den?
'Twas so; but this, all pleasure's fancies be.
If ever any beauty I did see,
Which I desired, and got, 'twas but a dream of thee.

And now good morrow to our waking souls,
   Which watch not one another out of fear;
For love, all love of other sights controls,
   And makes one little room, an every where.
Let sea-discoverers to new worlds have gone,
Let maps to others, worlds on worlds have shown,
Let us possess one world, each hath one and is one.

My face in thine eyes, thine in mine appears,
   And true plain hearts do in the faces rest,
Where can we find two better hemispheres
   Without sharp north, without declining west?
What ever dies, was not mixed equally;
If our two loves be one, or, thou and I
Love so alike, that none do slacken, none can die.

I am absolutely delighted to be in Christopher Wren's great Octagon Room in the original building of the Royal Observatory built in 1675. Sitting here I think of the great Astronomers Royal of Greenwich and I think in particular of the one whom I consider to be the greatest of them all, Edmund Halley. He was made Astronomer Royal in 1720, very near to the end of his life. He was an amazing person, he spent some of his life studying astronomy, but a great deal of his life adventuring, being a diplomat, being a bon viveur, being a classicist, a translator, an editor. I find one of the most exciting enterprises of my life was to have been very involved in communicating astronomy to the public when Halley's comet last visited earth on its seventy-six-year cycle. Every time I gave a talk about it or went on a radio programme people would say to me 'Why is Halley's name given to a comet that he didn't actually discover?' Well, Halley was the first person to make the prediction that a comet might not be, as it were, a flash in the pan but something which came back again and again. In his writings he makes it very clear that he has noted a comet which came by on several occasions and he predicts it's going to come back again. For that reason we honour that comet and Halley today.

Synopsis on the Astronomy of Comets (1705)
EDMUND HALLEY

For having collected all the Observations of Comets I could, I framed a table, the result of a prodigious deal of Calculation, which, tho' but small in Bulk, will be no unnacceptable present to Astronomers. For those Numbers are capable of Representing all that has been yet observed about the Motion of Comets, by the Help only of the following General Table; in the making of which I spared no Labour, that it might come forth perfect, as a Thing consecrated to Posterity, and to last as long as Astronomy itself.

The principal use therefore of this Table of the Elements . . . is, that whenever a new Comet shall appear, we may be able to know, by comparing together the Elements, whether it be any of those which has appeared before, and consequently . . . to foretell its Return. There are many Things which make me believe that the Comet . . . of 1531 was the same as that described in the Year 1607 and which I myself have seen return, and observed in the year 1682. All the Elements agree, and nothing seems to contradict this my Opinion . . . HENCE I DARE VENTURE TO FORETELL, THAT IT WILL RETURN AGAIN IN THE YEAR 1758. And, if it should then return, we shall have no Reason to doubt but the rest must return too.

Good old Halley. He got it right. It did come back in 1758; he would have been 112 years old. He lived to the ripe old age of 85, by the way. I understand he died with a glass of red wine in his hand. I don't think he'd be at all affronted if I included a sample of the kind of things people were saying about Halley's comet when it came here on its last but one return in 1910.

Tails
JAMES RAVENSCROFT

Tim O'Mara was conversing with his old pal, Mike Muldoon,
About the Halley comet while they gazed upon the moon,
'A comet's sure a wonder' said O'Mara, looking wise,
'It is,' Muldoon assented, 'An' the greatest in th' skies!
An' think of all th' books an' things the high-brow fellys write
About the strange beoggerfee of that celestial sight!'
Said O'Mara: 'For live writin's stuff the comet'll never fail,
And think of all it is because thereon hangs a tale.'

A Line-O-Type or Two
THE CHICAGO TRIBUNE

At a special meeting of the Chicago General Committee for the reception of Halley's Comet, Prof. Graham Taylor read a report from his Oxford colleague, Prof. Turner, stating that we shall all be in the tail of the comet May 18 and if we wish to bottle some of the air that day we can hand a part of the comet down to our grandchildren. On behalf of the Committee the Treasurer was instructed to purchase fifty dozen quarts of champagne for May 18. These, after being emptied, will be filled with Halley's best.

The St James's Gazette for April 16

In an essay on Halley's Comet, a Bavarian schoolboy wrote 'In this country the Comet has already caused a rise in the price of beer, but it may cause even greater misfortunes in other countries.'

41

Comet Mania
THE OBSERVATORY APRIL 1910

Oh, you Mistuh Comet,
   Travelin' th'oo de sky
You's got us all a-tremble
   As you comes a-brushin' by
We don' know what you's up to
   An' we don't know whah you's bin,
Nor whah you is a-gwineter.
   You's jes a-buttin' in!

Look here, Mistuh Comet,
   As on yoh way you ride,
You ain't much in partic'lar,
   An' mos'ly gassified.
You's like some folks I knows of
   Dat raises heaps o'fuss
Wifout a-bein' nuffin
   Except Mysterious.

After Halley's comet and all the great interest it generated I spend
my time at the moment tramping around the world and everywhere I go I get asked all kinds of questions about astronomy. Of
course the obvious one is 'What's a black hole?' The second most
common is 'Why are we here? What's life in the universe doing on
this planet?' It must be a question that can be replied to in so many
different ways, religious, philosophical and scientific. But of
course *With Great Pleasure* the only possible way is poetic. I
was delighted to be sent a poem from Michael Burnett of Dorset
which sums up so beautifully why there is life on this planet.

We Need a Star
MICHAEL BURNETT

We need a star that's fairly bright;
(Not too dark nor yet too light)
Not too big or brilliant blue;
Nor too red or feeble too.
We need one most that's by itself.
(Did fate leave it on the shelf?)

Doubles or triples just won't do
They make their planets go askew;
One day's too cold, the next's too hot,
Life's prospects there aren't worth a lot.
Our ideal, then, is 'medium yellow'
(And certainly a single fellow.)

A planet next, and fairly small,
One too big won't do at all;
For ones too big have forces that
Will tend to make things rather flat.
Yet one *too* small's no good, I fear,
'Cos it can't hold no atmosphere.
So, like its star, its girth should fall
Between the outsize and the small.
Next, it needs an orbit so's
It won't get burnt and won't get froze.
And if all this seems quite enough
Its make-up needs the 'proper stuff'.

Our nice round world, with gentle spin,
Needs atmosphere that's fairly thin.
It needs above all this, for sure,
An ozone layer to shut the door
On tissue-rending ultra-V
And then, below this too, some sea.
(It needs the sea for life depends
On water, water without end.)
Clouds – then lightning; strike the placid
Sleep of that amino-acid.
Now, wait five thousand million years.
And lo! Old Patrick Moore appears!

Readers: Timothy West, Kika Markham

Full Selection:
The Animal's Prayer, ENID BLYTON
Nature Notes, ENID BLYTON
Guide to the Stars, PATRICK MOORE

43

O Moon, ATTRIBUTED TO A MAID IN THE SERVICE OF THE
17TH-CENTURY ASTRONOMER CHRISTIAAN HUYGHENS
Middlesex, JOHN BETJEMAN
The Universe, ISAAC ASIMOV
Your Years of Toil, GEORGE GAMOW
Woman's Constancy, JOHN DONNE
The Good Morrow, JOHN DONNE
Great Central Railway – Sheffield Victoria to Banbury, JOHN
    BETJEMAN
King's England, ARTHUR MEE
Extract from Kilvert's Diary
Henry Moore's Sheep Sketchbook, HENRY MOORE (with
    introduction by LORD CLARK)
Ode to Autumn, JOHN KEATS
Synopsis on the Astronomy of Comets, EDMUND HALLEY
Tails, JAMES RAVENSCROFT
A Line-O-Type or Two, CHICAGO TRIBUNE
Essay on Halley's Comet, ST JAMES'S GAZETTE
The Comet, THE OBSERVATORY
We Need a Star, MICHAEL BURNETT

RICHARD CROSSMAN

1971

*For the first thirty years of his life the late Richard Crossman was devoted
to literature. A writer, teacher and would-be poet he thought of almost
nothing else. In common with many of his generation, the war changed
everything. He emerged a man of action, to whom politics were everything and literature 'just something there as a background'. As a
government minister his reading was largely a matter of whatever was*

delivered in those little red boxes. In consequence his choices were mainly from the 1920s and '30s which he had read when they first came out – chosen because 'they were all, in a sense, presentiments of the shape of things to come.'

The first thing I remember my mother reading to me deeply influenced my life. It was *Bleak House* by Charles Dickens, a tremendous book about a terrible law case and the people involved in it. My father was a Chancery Lawyer, and I don't know whether my mother realized it, but the reading of it to me made one thing quite sure: I would never become a lawyer.

Bleak House
CHARLES DICKENS

London. Michaelmas Term lately over, and the Lord Chancellor sitting in Lincoln's Inn Hall. Implacable November weather. As much mud in the streets, as if the waters had but newly retired from the face of the earth, and it would not be wonderful to meet a Megalosaurus, forty feet long or so, waddling like an elephantine lizard up Holborn Hill.

Fog everywhere. Fog up the river, where it flows along green aits and meadows; fog down the river, where it rolls defiled among the tiers of shipping, and the waterside pollutions of the great (and dirty) city. Fog on the Essex marshes, fog on the Kentish heights. Fog creeping into the cabooses of collier brigs; fog lying out on the yards, and hovering in the riggings of great ships; fog drooping on the gunwales of barges and small boats. Chance people on the bridges peeping over the parapets into a nether sky of fog, with fog all round them, as if they were up in a balloon, and hanging in the misty clouds.

The raw afternoon is rawest, and the dense fog is densest, and the muddy streets are muddiest, near that leaden-headed old obstruction, appropriate ornament for the threshold of a leaden-headed old corporation: Temple Bar. And hard by Temple Bar, in Lincoln's Inn Hall, at the very heart of the fog, sits the Lord High Chancellor in his High Court of Chancery.

Of course, home isn't the place where the biggest impressions come. So I move on quickly to school. I went to Winchester. You may think of Winchester as a place of conventional Wykenham-ists, but as a matter of fact it was for me a place of rebellion. I learnt to rebel against everything my parents taught me. My clearest memories of Winchester are not what I was taught in the class. In my first year I was the little fag who looked after Anthony Asquith, the son of Lady Asquith and, later, the distinguished film director. Under him we had readings of plays every Satur-day. I was the leading lady, you'll be surprised to hear, in all the Chekhov plays long before they were produced in London because Anthony Asquith was reading all the latest things. There was nothing we didn't read in those days together. And naturally my favourite poet, I needn't tell you, because I'd been brought up very religious, was Swinburne. So I have to ask you to excuse me for a passage from *A Hymn to Proserpine*, because it did in a way form a kind of challenge in my life.

Hymn to Proserpine
SWINBURNE

Oh Gods, dethroned and deceased, cast forth, wiped in a day!
From your wrath is the world released, redeemed from your
  chains, men say.
New Gods are crowned in the city; their flowers have broken
  your rods;
They are merciful, clothed with pity, the young compassionate
  Gods.
But for me their new device is barren, the days are bare;
Things long past over suffice, and men forgotten that were.
Time and the Gods are at strife; ye dwell in the midst thereof,
Draining a little life from the barren breasts of love.
Thou hast conquered, O pale Galilean; the world has grown
  grey from thy breath;
We have drunken of things Lethean, and fed on the fullness of
  death.

I went to Oxford and wanted to become a poet. I began to read almost nothing but poetry and I used to take a paper called the *New Criterion* which was edited by T. S. Eliot. In one number I remember there came out the first poem which captured me. I knew that I had discovered a poem, I knew what this poem meant to me and meant to the author. You'll be puzzled – it's a poem about an old man feeling old. I was a boy of twenty, but I felt very old. I've got a good deal younger since, I think. But I felt desperately old, desperately part of the establishment.

The Tower
W. B. YEATS

I
What shall I do with this absurdity –
O heart, O troubled heart – this caricature,
Decrepit age that has been tied to me
As to a dog's tail?

Never had I more
Excited, passionate, fantastical
Imagination, more an ear and eye
That more expected the impossible –
No, not in boyhood when with rod and fly,
Or the humbler worm, I climbed Ben Bulben's back
And had the livelong summer day to spend.

It seems that I must bid the Muse go pack,
Choose Plato and Plotinus for a friend
Until imagination, ear and eye,
Can be content with argument and deal
In abstract things; or be derided by
A sort of battered kettle at the heel.

III
It is time that I wrote my will;
I choose upstanding men,
That climb the streams until
The fountain leap, and at dawn
Drop their cast at the side
Of dripping stone; I declare
They shall inherit my pride. . . .
As at the loophole there,

The daws chatter and scream,
And drop twigs layer upon layer,
When they have mounted up,
The mother bird will rest
On their hollow top,
And so warm her wild nest.

I leave both faith and pride
To young upstanding men
Climbing the mountain side,
That under bursting dawn
They may drop a fly;
Being of that metal made
Till it was broken by
This sedentary trade,
Now shall I make my soul
Compelling it to study
In a learned school
Till the wreck of body
Slow decay of blood,
Testy delirium
Or dull decrepitude,
Or what worse evil come –
The death of friends, or death
Of every brilliant eye
That made a catch in the breath –
Seem but the clouds of the sky
When the horizon fades;
Or a bird's sleepy cry
Among the deepening shades.

Yeats, Eliot, Gerard Manley Hopkins and D. H. Lawrence were the great people in my life then, they were more real to me than anyone else. The other person was Wystan Auden. We were undergraduates together and at that time I was writing poems like Wystan Auden – I don't say they were as good, but you couldn't I don't think very much distinguish between them. The Auden of that period was very different from the portentous, famous poet he later became. In a way he was a divine fool with tremendous passion and a wonderful new idea of poetry. Here first is a love poem by him, a love poem about a boy.

Funeral Blues
W. H. AUDEN

Stop all the clocks, cut off the telephone,
Prevent the dog from barking with a juicy bone,
Silence the pianos and with muffled drum
Bring out the coffin, let the mourners come.

Let aeroplanes circle moaning overhead
Scribbling on the sky the message He Is Dead,
Put crepe bows round the white necks of the public doves
Let the traffic policemen wear black cotton gloves.

He was my North, my South, my East and West,
My working week and my Sunday rest,
My noon, my midnight, my talk, my song;
I thought that love would last forever: I was wrong.

The stars are not wanted now: put out every one,
Pack up the moon and dismantle the sun,
Pour away the ocean and sweep up the woods;
For nothing now can ever come to any good.

A sad poem, but now we'll take another bit of Auden. He was a great satirist in those days and I have to tell you that the next poem is one he's trying to have removed from his collected works because he thinks it's too shocking and too sharp. But it's a poem which reminds me of the mood of Oxford and of Berlin under the Weimar Republic.

Miss Gee
W. H. AUDEN

Let me tell you a little story
About Miss Edith Gee;
She lived in Clevedon Terrace
At number 83.

49

Miss Gee knelt down in the side-aisle,
She knelt down on her knees;
'Lead me not into temptation
But make me a good girl, please.'

She bicycled down to the doctor,
And rang the surgery bell;
'O, doctor, I've a pain inside me,
And I don't feel very well.'

Doctor Thomas looked her over,
And then he looked some more;
Walked over to his wash-basin,
Said, 'Why didn't you come before?'

Doctor Thomas sat over his dinner,
Though his wife was waiting to ring;
Rolling his bread into pellets,
Said 'Cancer's a funny thing.

'Nobody knows what the cause is,
Though some pretend they do;
It's like some hidden assassin
Waiting to strike at you.'

His wife she rang for the servant,
Said, 'Don't be so morbid, dear.'
He said; 'I saw Miss Gee this evening
And she's a gonner, I fear.'

They took Miss Gee to the hospital,
She lay there a total wreck,
Lay in the ward for women
With the bedclothes right up to her neck.

They laid her on the table,
The students began to laugh;
And Mr Rose the surgeon
He cut Miss Gee in half.

Mr Rose he turned to his students,
Said, 'Gentlemen, if you please,

We seldom see a sarcoma
As far advanced as this.'

They took her off the table,
They wheeled away Miss Gee
Down to another department
Where they study Anatomy.

They hung her from the ceiling,
Yes, they hung up Miss Gee;
And a couple of Oxford Groupers
Carefully dissected her knee.

I told you it was a bit sharp and it reminds me of the sharpness of
the Berlin Germany of that time. I went to live in Germany then
for a year and almost the first week I was there I went to the Opera
at Frankfurt-am-Main for the first night of a new opera by two
men who were not very well known outside Germany at that
time, Kurt Weill and Bertolt Brecht. The opera was *The Rise and
Fall of the City of Mahagonny*, and at the end of the first act there
were so many stink-bombs being thrown by the Nazis in the
gallery that the performance had to be stopped. As I walked
home a great Nazi procession came past me with torches. When I
got home that night I had a book I was reading by D. H. Lawrence
called *Fantasia of the Unconscious*. It's a book about psychoanalysis.
I'd reached a chapter called 'Trees and Babies and Papas and
Mammas' which I read that night. It really deeply shaped my life
and it may influence you.

Fantasia of the Unconscious
D. H. LAWRENCE

I listen again for noises, and I smell the damp moss. The looming
trees, so straight. And I listen for their silence – big, tall-bodied
trees, with a certain magnificent cruelty about them – or barbarity
– I don't know why I should say cruelty. Their magnificent,
strong, round bodies! It almost seems I can hear the slow, powerful sap drumming in their trunks. Great full-blooded trees, with
strange tree-blood in them soundlessly drumming.

I come so well to understand tree-worship. All the old Aryans worshipped the tree. My ancestors. The tree of life. The tree of knowledge. Well, one is bound to sprout out some time or other, chip off the old Aryan block. I can so well understand tree-worship, and fear the deepest motive.

Naturally. This marvellous vast individual without a face, without lips or eyes or heart. This towering creature that never had a face. Here am I between his toes like a pea-bug, and him noiselessly over-reaching me, and I feel his great blood-jet surging. And he has no eyes. But he turns two ways: he thrusts himself tremendously down to the middle earth, where dead men sink in darkness, in the damp, dense undersoil; and he turns himself about in high air; whereas we have eyes on one side of our head only, and only grow upwards.

And I can so well understand the Romans, their terror of the bristling Hercynian wood. Yet when you look from a height down upon the rolling of the forest – this Black Forest – it is as suave as a rolling, oily sea. Inside only, is bristles horrifice. And it terrified the Romans.

The Romans and the Greeks found everything human. Everything had a face, and a human voice. Men spoke, and their fountains piped an answer.

But when the legions crossed the Rhine they found a vast impenetrable life which had no voice. They met the faceless silence of the Black Forest. This huge, huge wood did not answer when they called. Its silence was too crude and massive. And the soldiers shrank: shrank before the trees that had no faces, and no answer.

No wonder the soldiers were terrified. No wonder they thrilled with horror when, deep in the woods, they found the skulls and trophies of their dead comrades upon the trees. The trees had devoured them: silently, in mouthfuls, and left the white bones. Bones of the mindful Romans – and savage, preconscious trees, indomitable. The true German has something of the sap of trees in his veins even now: He is a tree soul, and his gods are not human. His instinct still is to nail skulls and trophies to the sacred tree, deep in the forest. The tree of life and death, tree of good and evil, tree of abstraction and of immense, mindless life.

Readers: Denis Goucher, Denys Hawthorne

Full Selection:
Bleak House, CHARLES DICKENS
Hymn to Proserpine, ALGERNON CHARLES SWINBURNE
Plato Today, R. H. S. CROSSMAN
The Tower, W. B. YEATS
Funeral Blues, W. H. AUDEN
Miss Gee, W. H. AUDEN
Fantasia of the Unconscious, D. H. LAWRENCE
The Choice Before the Labour Party, R. H. TAWNEY
Sent to Coventry, GEORGE HODGKINSON
Romance, W. J. TURNER
2001: A Space Odyssey, ARTHUR C. CLARKE

PROFESSOR BARRY CUNLIFFE

1983

Many of those invited to present 'With Great Pleasure' begin with an account of being read to on a mother's or a father's knee. Professor Cunliffe on the other hand makes no bones about the fact that his childhood was un-literary. He hardly read anything until the age of twelve, preferring to spend the time roaming the fields around his uncle's farm. One day he learned that next to the farm had been a Roman villa. From then on he spent hours and hours kicking over the mole hills in search of Roman pot shards, picking up the tessiary that made up the mosaic pavements. It was a gentle introduction to what was to become his *lifelong passion, archaeology. Fortunately for the programme he later developed other passions, including reading and second-hand bookshops.*

I spend a very considerable part of each working year actually involved in excavation, two to three months, and for me each archaeological site takes on a character, and it's almost invariably the character of a woman. This is a very sexist thing to say, but I can't help feeling that the relationship of an excavation director to a site is rather like that of a man to a woman – the woman has to be cared for and cajoled into showing her secrets. It will probably ruin my chances of appearing on 'Woman's Hour', but nevertheless I do actually feel that. I feel it in particular about Bath, beneath the Pump Room, right in the heart of the temple dedicated to Sulis Minerva the goddess of Wisdom, the goddess of hearing. Every excavation produces wonderful experiences and surprises, and one of the surprises, egg on the faces of all the archaeologists working on it, was when we discovered temple steps where we were not expecting to find them. I thought a cellar had cut them away – a trench was dug to put a sewer in – but the cellar hadn't cut them away: there they were. I had to explain it quickly, why we were wrong, and then to explain to the press how very much we wanted to preserve those steps, but we didn't have any money to do it; we'd probably just have to fill the hole in and roof it over, but if we could get the money we would be able to make them open to the public. Within two days I received a letter:

Letter from Children of Twerton School

Dear Professor Cunliffe,
The children in this school are trying to save some money to help keep the temple steps where people can see them. Some of us are giving money instead of buying sweets and comics. We have collected £1-75p in two days. We have some other ideas as well. How soon will you be needing our money? We hope you are successful in your digging and getting the money for the steps.
Yours sincerely
The Children of Twerton C. of E. School
(Newton Road, Twerton, Bath: 12th February 1981)

It's quite the nicest letter I've ever received. Now there is a tail piece to that story: the money *was* raised, the children handed over their cheque, the steps were protected and the first members of the general public to see the steps were the children of that school.

In the 8th century AD, a Saxon poet stood more or less where we were excavating beneath the Pump Room and he looked around and he saw this great decaying Roman building. What he would have seen, I think, was the chamber in which the sacred spring was, where the King's bath now is. The walls were standing and the roof was still there, a tiled roof although the tiles were falling off. The portico had fallen down in a great tumble of rubble and he got to thinking, presumably, about the transience of life and the inconsequence of man. He wrote a poem and the remarkable thing is that a substantial part of that poem still survives.

The Ruin
Translated from Old English by
KEVIN CROSSLEY-HOLLAND

Wondrous is this stone wall, wrecked by fate;
the city buildings crumble, the works of giants decay.
Roofs have caved in, towers collapsed,
barred gates are broken, hoar frost clings to mortar,
houses are gaping, tottering and fallen,
undermined by age. The earth's embrace,
its fierce grip, holds the mighty craftsmen;
they are perished and gone. A hundred generations
have passed away since then. This wall, grey with lichen
and red of hue, outlives kingdom after kingdom,
withstands tempests; its tall gate succumbed.
The city still smoulders, gashed by storms. . . .

A man's mind quickened with a plan;
subtle and strong-willed, he bound
the foundations with metal rods – a marvel.
Bright were the city halls, many the bath-houses,
lofty all the gables, great the martial clamour,
many a mead-hall was full of delights

until fate the mighty altered it. Slaughtered men
fell far and wide, the plague-days came,
death removed every brave man.
Their ramparts became abandoned places,
the city decayed; warriors and builders
fell to the earth. Thus these courts crumble,
and this redstone arch sheds tiles.

The place falls to ruin, shattered
into mounds of stone, where once many a man,
joyous and gold-bright, dressed in splendour,
proud and flush with wine, gleamed in his armour;
he gazed on his treasure – silver, precious stones,
jewellery and wealth, all that he owned –
and on this bright city in the broad kingdom.
Stone houses stood here; a hot spring
gushed in a wide stream; a stone wall
enclosed the bright interior; the baths
were here, the heated water; that was convenient.
They allowed the scalding water to pour
over the grey stone into the circular pool.

Apart from excavating, I also spend a very considerable amount
of time travelling abroad and it's something I enormously enjoy. I
also enjoy the peculiarity of foreigners. This has produced the
most substantial and extremely amusing literature, and I'm
always surprised at how often things noted in the past are still
very much true today.

If you drive through any part of France you'll be extremely
aware, I think, of the Frenchman's love of shooting any living
thing that moves. I remember driving through one part of France
on a Sunday morning and I was absolutely convinced that the
birds were actually using the car as cover, to get from one bunch
of shooters to another. Exactly the same preoccupation was
beautifully noted by Tobias Smollett in 1776.

Travels Through France and Italy
TOBIAS SMOLLETT

In the character of the French, considered as a people, there are
undoubtedly many circumstances truly ridiculous. You know the

PROFESSOR BARRY CUNLIFFE

fashionable people, who go hunting, are equipped with their jack boots, bag wigs, swords and pistols: but I saw the other day a scene still more grotesque. On the road to Choissi, a fiacre, or hackney-coach, stopped, and out came five or six men, armed with musquets, who took post, each behind a separate tree. I asked our servant who they were, imagining they might be archers, or footpads of justice, in pursuit of some malefactor. But guess my surprise, when the fellow told me, they were gentlemen à la chasse (out hunting). They were in fact come out from Paris, in this equipage, to take the diversion of hare-hunting; that is, of shooting from behind a tree at the hares that chanced to pass. Indeed, if they had nothing more in view, but to destroy the game, this was a very effectual method; for the hares are in such plenty in this neighbourhood, that I have seen a dozen together, in the same field. I think this way of hunting, in a coach or chariot, might be properly adopted at London, in favour of those aldermen of the city, who are too unwieldy to follow the hounds a-horseback.

I think that's a fair comment on those who kill things and call it fun.

Now one of the very exciting things I always find about archaeology is that I have to deal with sites or individual monuments about which people have written in the past, and to look at those sites in relation to the words that have been written about them is a remarkable experience.

In Athens away from all the dreadful tourists' tat and trouble and away from all those filthy petrol fumes, in so far as you can actually get away from petrol fumes in Athens, tucked away in a side street there's a small archaeological excavation which very few people go to. It's now known as Karonikos. If you look there you can see the city wall of Athens a few blocks high running across and a gate. Leading to that gate are two roads, and alongside those roads is a cemetery, a cemetery of the ancient Athenians, and it was here that in the 5th century BC Pericles gathered together all the citizens of Athens and addressed them. It was a moving occasion, a funeral oration given for the young men who had died saving Athens from Spartan totalitarianism. One of the things that Pericles did was to emphasize the nature of

57

democracy. It is, I think, one of the finest pieces of writing on the nature of democracy ever.

Quotation From Pericles

Let me say that our system of government does not copy the institutions of our neighbours. It is more a case of our being a model to others than of our imitating anyone else. Our Constitution is called a democracy because power is in the hands not of the minority but of the whole people. When it is a question of settling private disputes everyone is equal before the law. When it is a question of putting one person before another in positions of public responsibility what counts is not membership of a particular class but the actual ability which a man possesses. No one so long as he has it in him to be of service to the State is kept in political obscurity because of poverty. We give our obedience to those whom we put in positions of authority and we obey the laws themselves. Especially those who offer the protection of the oppressed. Our love of what is beautiful doesn't lead to extravagance, our love of things of the mind doesn't make us soft. We regard wealth as something to be properly used rather than something to boast about. As for poverty, no one need be ashamed to admit it. You must yourselves realise the power of Athens and feast your eyes upon her from day to day and become her lovers. And when all her greatness shall break upon you, you must reflect that it was by courage, sense of duty and a keen feeling of honour in action that men were able to win all this.

I confess that the enjoyment of food and wine is another of my passions. I think Hilaire Belloc got his priorities absolutely correct when, addressing an after-dinner speech to some friends after they had had a very good meal indeed, he ended up by saying 'When that this too too solid flesh shall melt away and I am called before my Heavenly Father I shall say to him Sire, I don't remember the name of the village and I don't remember the name of the girl, but the wine was Chambertin.'

He actually said that at the Saintsbury Club – a meeting of this very famous club that was founded in honour of a remarkable man, George Saintsbury. He was Regius Professor of Rhetoric at Edinburgh University. Whether he was any good at rhetoric I've no idea, but he is extremely well-known for his legendary love of wine.

Notes on a Cellar Book
GEORGE SAINTSBURY

It was really a wonderful wine. This was a Red Hermitage of 1846. When the last bottle was put on the table it showed not the slightest mark or presage of enfeeblement, but it was the manliest French wine I ever drank. You had to be careful of it in some ways; one of the best-known of all my friends had very remarkable experiences as a consequence of neglecting my warnings, and consuming whisky instead of brandy with his soda after it. But there is no good in any man, woman or wine that will allow liberties to be taken with them. To champagne before it, it had no objection; nor, as hinted just now, to brandy afterwards. But it was uncompromisingly Gallic in its patriotism.

Readers: Angela Down, Peter Jeffrey

Full Selection:
Memories of Christmas, DYLAN THOMAS
Emily Writes Such a Good Letter, STEVIE SMITH
Lenten Thoughts of a High Anglican, JOHN BETJEMAN
The Return of the Native, THOMAS HARDY
Letter from Children of Twerton School
The Ruin, trans. KEVIN CROSSLEY-HOLLAND
Travels Through France and Italy, TOBIAS SMOLLETT
Senility, LLYWARCH HEN
Warning, JENNY JOSEPH
Let Me Die a Youngman's Death, ROGER McGOUGH
Rome in Africa, SIMON RAVEN
The Odyssey, HOMER
The Portable Swift, JONATHAN SWIFT
Quotation From Pericles
Notes on a Cellar Book, GEORGE SAINTSBURY
Coming Down from the Chung-Nan Mountain, LI PO

MARGARET DRABBLE

1979

'I loved tragedy and wasn't very good at seeing jokes.' That was Margaret Drabble's brisk summing-up of herself as a child, and perhaps more than most her edition of 'With Great Pleasure' harked back to her childhood. Indeed, it was recorded at her old school, The Mount, in York. Since her time there she has, of course, learnt to enjoy jokes, and she included many in her selection. However, through the good humour and the enjoyment of adult pleasures there is a hint of wistfulness for the state of childhood itself, as if the party had ended too soon, before the last round of 'pass the parcel', the cake unfinished and the going-home present uncertain.

I read a great deal while I was at school, I read licitly in the classroom and illicitly in boiler rooms and in bed with a torch under the bedclothes, and I can honestly say that I remember even the set texts we did in English for O' level and A' level with the greatest pleasure. But my passion for reading pre-dated my arrival at The Mount. All our family were great readers when I was little, and we all still are. My mother never censored our reading in any way; she encouraged us to read anything in the house or that we could find in the Sheffield Public Library. One of my earliest favourites was a book called *The Golden Windows* by Laura Richards, which I think was a Sunday School prize of one of my parents. I loved these fables, but lost sight of them for years when the book disappeared during one of the family's removals. I was delighted to find a copy of this rather rare book in a second-hand bookshop in Salisbury one sunny day a few years ago, and when I reread the stories I found them even more touching than I'd done as a child. This is one that I'd remembered with great clarity, and of which I often think as I watch my own children, two of them now larger than me, striding forth into the world.

The Blind Mother
LAURA RICHARDS

A blind woman had a son, who was the joy of her life. Though she had no sight of her eyes, yet she was skilful of her hands; and it was her delight to make pretty clothes for her boy, soft and fine and full of delicate stitches.

By and by the boy came to her and said: 'Mother, give me some other clothes to wear. These are too small for me; they pinch and bind me. Moreover, they are baby clothes, and my play-fellows mock and laugh at me because of them.'

But the mother said: 'Nay, my darling; these are by far the best clothes for you. See how soft and warm they are! They are pretty too, I know, although I cannot see them. Be content, for you are my own darling little son, and so you must remain.'

When he found he could not persuade her, the boy held his peace; and he went out and looked about him, and found the hide of a wolf and the pelt of a fox, and huddled them round him over his baby frock, and so went among his mates. Only, when he came back to the room where his mother sat, he threw aside the skins, and came to her in his frock; and she kissed him, and felt the frills and silken stitches, and said rejoicing: 'You are my own darling little son, and the light of my life.'

By and by again there was a war in that country, and all the young men went out to meet the enemy. Some were clad in the armour of proof, others in leathern jacks and doublets; and with them went the son of the blind woman.

Then when the woman knew that her son was gone, she wept and lamented, and ran out into the street. There she met one who was returning from the field of battle, and she asked him how went the fight.

'Bravely', he replied. 'Our men did well, all save one who had no arms, and whom I saw beaten down and at sore odds with the enemy.'

'Oh! stranger,' cried the blind woman, 'was that one a boy,

who had wandered by mistake into that dreadful field, – a sweet child, with the prettiest clothes, all wrought with needlework?'

'Nay', said the stranger. 'It was a man, half-naked, huddled in the skins of beasts, with strange rags showing under the skins.'

'Oh!' said the woman. 'I wonder who that poor soul might be; and I wonder when my little darling son will come home to me again.'

And even while she spoke her son lay dead, and huddled round him was the hide of a wolf and the pelt of a fox, with the baby clothes fluttering from under them.

As I said, I often think of that when my own children set off in their battle dresses, boiler suits, badges and armour plating, and I think that perhaps that's why they dress like that and I mustn't, as my son says, stifle them too much.

One of the most lasting legacies of my Mount days is an intimate knowledge of the contents of the *Songs of Praise*, which I used to feel was a sign of misspent meetings for worship, as too good a knowledge of billiards is said to be a sign of a misspent youth. But in the long run I think it is time well-spent, and hymns circulate round my head on occasions appropriate and inappropriate. Unfortunately I couldn't sing, though I learnt to mouth the words excellently to deceive Miss Birch in hymn practice – this is still a useful accomplishment during 'God Save the Queen'. One of my favourites, 'The Eternal Order', by Edward Grubb, still sums up my theological position (I believe Edward Grubb was a Quaker, related to Sarah Grubb, a founder of Ackworth School – one of the first real live poets I ever met was a relative named Frederick).

The Eternal Order
EDWARD GRUBB

Our God, to whom we turn
    When weary with illusion,
Whose stars serenely burn
    Above this earth's confusion,
Thine is the mighty plan,
    The steadfast order sure,

In which the world began,
    Endures, and shall endure.

Thou art thyself the Truth;
    Though we, who fain would find thee,
Have tried, with thoughts uncouth,
    In feeble words to bind thee,
It is because thou art
    We're driven to the quest;
Till truth from falsehood part
    Our souls can find no rest.

In my day we were taught Scripture by a teacher called Mrs
Webster, whom I remember vividly and with much affection. She
introduced us to arguments for and against the existence of God.
'And I rather think 'The Eternal Order,' she said, 'was an
illustration of the ontological argument in favour of the existence
of God.' And she said that was why I liked it. I remember that she
was surprised and I think a little disturbed to find me at the age of
sixteen deeply impressed by the pessimism of Thomas Hardy,
who seemed to me to have all the answers to life's meaningless-
ness. 'But don't you think it's *exaggerated*?' she would cry, as I
wept over *Jude the Obscure*, and now I see what she meant, but I
still love Hardy, and this poem, 'The Darkling Thrush', seems to
me to capture the essence of his peculiarly hopeful despair, as
well as presenting us with one of his finest landscapes.

The Darkling Thrush
THOMAS HARDY

I leant upon a coppice gate
    When Frost was spectre-gray,
And winter's dregs made desolate
    The weakening eye of day.
The tangled bine-stems scored the sky
    Like strings of broken lyres,
And all mankind that haunted nigh
    Had sought their household fires.

The land's sharp features seemed to be
    The Century's corpse outleant,

63

His crypt the cloudy canopy,
 The wind his death-lament.
The ancient pulse of germ and birth
 Was shrunken hard and dry,
And every spirit upon earth
 Seemed fervourless as I.

At once a voice arose among
 The bleak twigs overhead
In a full-hearted evensong
 Of joy illimited;
An aged thrush, frail, gaunt and small,
 In blast be-ruffled plume,
Had chosen thus to fling his soul
 Upon the growing gloom.

So little cause for carollings
 Of such ecstatic sound
Was written on terrestrial things
 Afar or nigh around,
That I could think there trembled through
 His happy good-night air
Some blessed Hope, whereof he knew
 And I was unaware.

It's amazing and rather frightening looking back to see what lasting and unexpected discoveries teachers can make for us and, as a teacher myself, I sometimes feel rather frightened about the influence I might be having and things I forget I've ever said come back to me in the most curious ways. The next poem was introduced to me by the then headmistress, Miss Garrick Smith, who found me crying on those stone steps which go up by the side of her study – I can't remember what I was crying about – and she took me into her study which at first rather terrified me than comforted me, and then she read me this wonderful Shakespeare sonnet which I now know by heart and which I often repeat to myself in times of stress.

Sonnet 29
WILLIAM SHAKESPEARE

When, in disgrace with fortune and men's eyes,
I all alone beweep my outcast state,
And trouble deaf heaven with my bootless cries,
And look upon myself, and curse my fate,
Wishing me like to one more rich in hope,
Featured like him, like him with friends possess'd,
Desiring this man's art, and that man's scope,
With what I most enjoy contented least;
Yet in these thoughts myself almost despising,
Haply I think on thee, and then my state,
Like to the lark at break of day arising
From sullen earth, sings hymns at heaven's gate:
  For thy sweet love rememb'red such wealth brings
  That then I scorn to change my state with kings.

What a comfort it is to reflect that even Shakespeare had moments when he desired other men's art and scope. And as for envying other men's features or other girls' features, I know that when I was a girl I'd willingly have changed my appearance with anybody in the school and used to envy everyone for the plain fact that they didn't look like me. I've got over that now, I think.

One of the great revelations of my early reading years was Emily Brontë. I came across *Wuthering Heights* when I was just the right age, about fourteen, and have loved it ever since. It is one of the great romantic novels, and it managed to communicate itself even to the most philistine of us in our fourth year. Emily Brontë has also written some of the great love poetry, which is one of literature's paradoxes – how can she have known about love, living as she did so cut off from the world? I think the metaphysical quality of her yearning gives the poetry a terrible intensity, which in its way is as comforting as Shakespeare's sonnet. I've never worked out why the expression of intense emotion, even of the most painful variety, should be consoling, but it is so.

The Appeal
EMILY BRONTË

If grief for grief can touch thee,
    If answering woe for woe,
If any ruth can melt thee,
    Come to me now!

I cannot be more lonely,
    More drear I cannot be!
My worn heart throbs so wildly,
    'Twill break for thee.

And when the world despises,
    When Heaven repels my prayer,
Will not mine angel comfort?
    Mine idol hear?

Yes, by the tears I've poured thee,
    By all my hours of pain,
Oh, I shall surely win thee,
    Beloved, again!

Arnold Bennett has long been one of my more eccentric pleasures. At Cambridge he was dismissed in a footnote, but I knew there was more to him than that. I enjoy everything he wrote, and he wrote plenty, but the great novels, *Clayhanger* and *The Old Wives' Tale*, seem to me to stand with the best novels in our literature. There is something in my own family background that responds to Arnold Bennett because in fact my mother's family came from the Potteries and claimed to be related to the Bennetts. Mind you, Bennett is a very common name, there are a lot of Bennetts in the Potteries, but we like to think that we're related to them and I recognize in particular the kind of social background that is described in this children's birthday party from *The Old Wives' Tale*.

The Old Wives' Tale
ARNOLD BENNETT

Cyril, while attending steadily to the demands of his body, was in a mood which approached the ideal. Proud and radiant, he combined urbanity with a certain fine condescension. His bright eyes, and his manner of scraping up jam with a spoon, said: 'I am the king of this party. This party is solely in my honour. I know that. We all know it. Still, I will pretend we are equals, you and I.' He talked about his picture-books to a young woman on his right named Jennie, aged four, pale, pretty, the belle in fact. The boy's attractiveness was indisputable; he could put on quite an aristocratic air. It was the most delicious sight to see them, Cyril and Jennie, so soft and delicate, so infantile on their piles of cushions and books, with their white socks and black shoes dangling far distant from the carpet; and yet so old, so self-contained!

And they were merely the epitome of the whole table. The whole table was bathed in the charm and mystery of young years, of helpless fragility, gentle forms, timid elegance, unshamed instincts, and waking souls. Constance and Samuel were very satisfied.

They both really did believe, at that moment, that Cyril was, in some subtle way which they both felt but could not define, superior to all other infants.

Someone, some officious relative of a visitor, began to pass a certain cake which had brown walls, a roof of coco-nut icing, and a yellow body studded with crimson globules. Not a conspicuously gorgeous cake, not a cake to which a catholic child would be likely to attach particular importance; a good average cake! Who could have guessed that it stood, in Cyril's esteem, as the cake of cakes? Now, by the hazard of destiny that cake found much favour, helped into popularity as it was by the blundering officious relative who, not dreaming what volcano she was treading on, urged its merits with simpering enthusiasm. One boy took two slices, a slice in each hand; he happened to be the visitor of whom the cake-distributor was a relative, and she protested; she expressed the shock she suffered. Whereupon both Constance and Samuel sprang forward and swore with angelic smiles that nothing could be more perfect than the propriety of that dear little fellow taking two slices of that cake. It was this hullaballoo that drew Cyril's attention to the evanescence of the cake of cakes. His face at once changed from calm pride to a dreadful anxiety. His eyes bulged out. His tiny mouth

67

grew and grew, like a mouth in a nightmare. He was no longer human; he was a cake-eating tiger balked of his prey. Nobody noticed him. The officious fool of a woman persuaded Jennie to take the last slice of the cake, which was quite a thin slice.

Then every one simultaneously noticed Cyril, for he gave a yell. It was not the cry of a despairing soul who sees his beautiful iridescent dream shattered at his feet: it was the cry of the strong, masterful spirit, furious. He turned upon Jennie, sobbing and snatched her cake. Unaccustomed to such behaviour from hosts, and being besides a haughty put-you-in-your-place beauty of the future, Jennie defended her cake. After all, it was not she who had taken two slices at once. Cyril hit her in the eye, and then crammed most of the slice of cake into his enormous mouth. He could not swallow it, nor even masticate it, for his throat was rigid and tight. So the cake projected from his red lips, and big tears watered it. The most awful mess you can conceive! Jennie wept loudly, and one or two others joined her in sympathy, but the rest went on eating tranquilly, unmoved by the horror which transfixed their elders.

A host to snatch food from a guest! A host to strike a guest! A gentleman to strike a lady!

Constance whipped up Cyril from his chair and flew with him to his own room, where she smacked him on the arm and told him he was a very, very naughty boy and that she didn't know what his father would say. She took the food out of his disgusting mouth – or as much of it as she could get at – and she left him, on the bed. Miss Jennie was still in tears when, blushing scarlet and trying to smile, Constance returned to the drawing-room. Jennie would not be appeased. Miss Insull had promised to see Jennie home, and it was decided that she should go. Then all pretended, and said loudly, that what had happened was naught, that such things were always happening at children's parties.

But the attempt to keep up appearance was a failure.

The Methuselah of visitors, a gaping girl of nearly eight years, walked across the room to where Constance was standing, and said in a loud, confidential, fatuous voice:

'Cyril *has* been a rude boy, hasn't he, Mrs Povey?'

Readers: Eleanor Bron, Edward Petherbridge

Full Selection:
The Blind Mother, LAURA M. RICHARDS
The Eternal Order, EDWARD GRUBB
Pride and Prejudice, JANE AUSTEN
The Darkling Thrush, THOMAS HARDY
Sonnet 29, WILLIAM SHAKESPEARE
The Appeal, EMILY BRONTË
The Mill on the Floss, GEORGE ELIOT
Anglo-Saxon Attitudes, ANGUS WILSON
The Prelude, Book VI, WILLIAM WORDSWORTH
Scoop, EVELYN WAUGH
Casanova's Chinese Restaurant, ANTHONY POWELL
Consolation, W. B. YEATS
Antony and Cleopatra, WILLIAM SHAKESPEARE
The Old Wives' Tale, ARNOLD BENNETT
Vacillation, W. B. YEATS

NELL DUNN

1983

Up the Junction, Poor Cow *and* Steaming, *plays about apparently ordinary people displaying great vitality in the face of an unjust society, have made Nell Dunn's reputation as a writer secure – not that one suspects she would give even a passing thought to such a thing as her reputation. On the evidence of her edition of 'With Great Pleasure' she is more concerned with the idea of properly taking stock of oneself, of achieving a proper understanding in a world where habit and custom could become an excuse for morality: responsible behaviour may be more*

69

correctly defined by an irresponsible act because it is more true to the person committing it than any amount of habitual virtue.

I had an exotic childhood. I travelled, and what I always longed for was ordinariness. I had a mother who was always singing arias from Richard Strauss or Verdi, who spoke about five languages, and knew everyone, when what I longed for was a mum in a pinny, with floury hands, who bustled around the kitchen. And yet, Athens and the Far East – yes, it sounds exciting – but how to get security and excitement, that is the question.

Clarissa by Samuel Richardson was written in 1748. Some call it the first English novel: written in the form of letters, it is about a young woman's fight to preserve her integrity and not to marry Mr Solmes – as Clarissa puts it, she cannot 'cajole, fawn upon and play the hypocrite with a man to whom I have an aversion'.

I feel it was Clarissa Harlow, and women like her, whose courage eventually won us the enormous freedom women enjoy today. We are not only free now to marry the men we love, but also free, if we don't wish to marry, to live with men and pay our own bills, to be independent women. Here then Clarissa, about to be trapped into politeness with her suitor, Mr Solmes, shows her boldness and proceeds to beg her mother to speak on her behalf to her father that she should not be forced to marry. It seems, even in the eighteenth century, the nicest families had problems.

Clarissa
SAMUEL RICHARDSON

My mother was angry enough without all that; and asked me to what purpose I came down, if I were still so untractable?

She had hardly spoken the words when Shorey came in to tell her that Mr Solmes was in the hall, and desired admittance.

Ugly creature! What, at the close of day, quite dark, had brought him hither? But, on second thoughts, I believe it was contrived, that he should be here at supper, to know the result of the conference between my mother and me, and that my father, on his return, might find us together.

I was hurrying away; but my mother commanded me (since I had come down only, as she said, to mock her) not to stir; and at the same time see if I could behave so to Mr Solmes, as might encourage her to make the favourable report to my father which I had besought her to make.

My sister triumphed. I was vexed to be caught, and to have such an angry and cutting rebuke given me, with an aspect more like the taunting sister than the indulgent mother, if I may presume to say so: for she herself seemed to enjoy the surprise upon me.

The man stalked in. His usual walk is by pauses, as if from the same vacuity of thought which made Dryden's clown whistle he was telling his steps, and first paid his clumsy respects to my mother; then to my sister; next to me as if I were already his wife, and therefore to be the last in his notice; and sitting down by me, told us in general what weather it was. Very cold he made it; but I was warm enough. Then addressing himself to me; and how do *you* find it, miss? was his question; and would have taken my hand.

I withdrew it, I believe with disdain enough. My mother frowned. My sister bit her lip.

I could not contain myself: I never was so bold in my life; for I went on with my plea as if Mr Solmes had not been there.

My mother coloured, and looked at him, at my sister, and at me. My sister's eyes were opener and bigger than I ever saw them before.

The man understood me. He hemmed, and removed from one chair to another.

I went on, supplicating for my mother's favourable report: Nothing but invincible dislike, said I –

What would the girl be at, interrupted my mother? Why Clary! Is this a subject! Is this! – is this! – is this a time – and again she looked upon Mr Solmes.

I am sorry, on reflection, that I put my mamma into so much confusion. To be sure it was very saucy in me.

I beg pardon, madam, said I. But my papa will soon return. And since I am not permitted to withdraw, it is not necessary, I humbly presume, that Mr Solmes's presence should deprive me of this opportunity to implore your favourable report; and at the same time, if he still visit on my account (looking at him) to convince him, that it cannot possibly be to any purpose –

Is the girl mad? said my mother, interrupting me.

My sister, with the affectation of a whisper to my mother: This is – this is *spite*, madam (very *spitefully* she spoke the word) because you commanded her to stay.

I only looked at her, and turning to my mother, Permit me, madam, said I, to repeat my request. I have no brother, no sister! If I lose my mamma's favour I am lost for ever!

Mr. Solmes removed to his first seat, and fell to knawing the head of his hazel; a carved head, almost as ugly as his own – I did not think the man was so *sensible*.

My sister rose, with a face all over scarlet, and stepping to the table, where lay a fan, she took it up, and although Mr. Solmes had observed that the weather was cold, fanned herself very violently.

My mother came to me, and angrily taking my hand, led me out of that parlour into my own; which, you know, is next to it. Is not this behaviour very bold, very provoking, think you, Clary?

Clarissa for me is a highly moral book. It tells us to think independently, feel independently, trust your own thoughts and feelings.

My father was a Master of Hounds, and *Memoirs of a Fox-Hunting Man* by Siegfried Sassoon was one of his favourite books. This extract is about a young boy's first hunt on his marvellous pony, Sheila, and I'd like to dedicate it to my own son, Gem, also a keen huntsman; and to my own childhood, whose happiest hours were spent with my sister and our beloved ponies in Savernake Forest on the Marlborough Downs.

Memoirs of a Fox-Hunting Man
SIEGFRIED SASSOON

'That's Mr Macdoggart,' said Dixon in a low voice, and my solemnity increased as the legendary figure vanished on its mysterious errand.

Meanwhile the huntsman was continuing his intermittent yaups as he moved along the other side to the wood. Suddenly his cheers of encouragement changed to a series of excited shoutings. 'Hoick-holler, hoick-holler, hoick-holler!' he yelled, and then blew his horn loudly; this was followed by an outbreak of vociferation from the hounds, and soon they were in full cry across the covert. I sat there petrified by my private feelings; Sheila showed no symptoms of agitation; she merely cocked her ears and listened.

And then, for the first time, I heard a sound which has thrilled generations of fox-hunters to their marrow. From the far side of the wood came the long shrill screech (for which it is impossible to find an adequate word) which signifies that one of the whips has viewed the fox quitting the covert. 'Gone away' it meant. But before I had formulated that haziest notion about it Lord Dumborough was galloping up the ride and the rest of them were pelting after him as though nothing could stop them. As I happened to be standing well inside the wood and Sheila took the affair into her own control, I was swept along with them, and we emerged on the other side among the leaders. I cannot claim that I felt either excitement or resolution as we bundled down a long slope of meadowland and dashed helter-skelter through an open gate at the bottom.

I knew nothing at all except that I was out of breath and that the air was rushing to meet me, but as I hung on to the reins I was aware that Mr Macdoggart was immediately in front of me. My attitude was an acquiescent one. I have always been inclined to accept life in the form in which it has imposed itself upon me, and on that particular occasion, no doubt, I just felt that I was 'in for it'. It did not so much as occur to me that in following Mr Macdoggart I was setting myself rather a high standard, and when he disappeared over the hedge I took it for granted that I must do the same. For a moment Sheila hesitated in her stride. (Dixon told me afterwards that I actually hit her as we approached the fence, but I couldn't remember having done so.) Then she collected herself and jumped the fence with a peculiar arching of her back. There was a considerable drop on the other side. Sheila had made no mistake, but as she landed I left the saddle and flew over her head. I had let go of the reins, but she stood stock-still while I sat on the wet ground.

I wanted to include a bit from the *Confessions* of Jean Jacques Rousseau, because it was my bible when I was about fifteen or sixteen. I learnt about intimacy from Rousseau – I mean I perhaps felt on more intimate terms with Rousseau then than with anybody I actually knew. I also learnt about the delicious foolishness of the human race.

Confessions
JEAN JACQUES ROUSSEAU

I entered the room of a courtesan as if it had been the sanctuary of love and beauty; in her person I thought I beheld its divinity. I should never have believed that, without respect and esteem, I should have experienced the emotions with which she inspired me. No sooner had I realised, in the preliminary familiarities, the value of her charms and caresses than, for fear of losing the fruit of them in advance, I was anxious to make haste and pluck it. Suddenly, in place of the flame which consumed me, I felt a deathly chill run through my veins; my legs trembled under me; and, feeling ready to faint, I sat down and cried like a child.

Who would guess the reason of my tears, and the thoughts which passed through my head at that moment? I said to myself: this object, which is at my disposal, is the masterpiece of nature and love; its mind and body, every part of it perfect; she is as good and generous as she is amiable and beautiful. The great ones of the world ought to be her slaves; sceptres ought to be laid at her feet. And yet she is a miserable street-walker, on sale to everybody; a merchant captain has the disposal of her; she comes and throws herself at my head, mine, although she knows that I am poor, while my real merits, being unknown to her, can have no value in her eyes. In this there is something incomprehensible. Either my heart deceives me, dazzles my senses, and makes me the dupe of a worthless slut, or some secret defect, with which I am unacquainted, must destroy the effect of her charms, and render her repulsive to those who would otherwise fight for the possession of her. I began to look for this defect with a singular intensity of mind, and it never occurred to me that the possible consequences of having anything to do with her might possibly have something to do with it. The freshness of her skin, her brilliant complexion, her dazzlingly white teeth, the sweetness of her breath, the general air of cleanliness about her whole person, so completely banished this idea from my mind, that, being still in doubt as to my condition since my visit to the padoana, I rather felt qualms of conscience as to whether I was in sufficiently good health for her, and I am quite convinced that I was not deceived in my confidence.

These well-timed reflections so agitated me that I shed tears. Zulietta, for whom this was certainly quite a novel sight, under the circumstances, was astounded for a moment; but, having walked round the room and looked in her glass, she understood, and my eyes convinced her, that dislike had nothing to do with this whimsical melancholy. It was an easy matter for her to drive it away, and to efface the slight feeling of shame; but, at the moment when I was ready to sink exhausted upon a bosom, which seemed to permit for the first time the contact of a man's hand and mouth, I perceived that she had only one nipple. I smote my forehead, looked attentively and thought I saw that this nipple was not formed like the other. I immediately began to rack my brains for the reason for such a defect, and, feeling convinced that it was connected with some remarkable natural imperfection, by brooding so long over this idea, I saw, as clear as daylight, that, in the place of the most charming person that I could picture to myself, I only held in my arms a kind of monster, the outcast of nature, of mankind and of love. I pushed my stupidity so far as to speak to her about this defect. At first she took it as a joke, and said and did things in her frolicsome humour, which were enough to make me die of love; but as I was unable to conceal from her that I still felt a certain amount of uneasiness, she at last blushed, adjusted her dress, got up, and, without saying a word, went and seated herself at the window. I wanted to sit by her side, but she moved, sat down on a couch, got up immediately afterwards, and, walking about the room and fanning herself, said to me in a cold and disdainful tone, 'Zanetto, lascia de donne, et studia la matematica.'

(Give up the ladies, and study mathematics.)

Readers: Geoffrey Palmer, Caroline Blakiston

Full Selection:
The Unquiet Grave, CYRIL CONNOLLY
Louise, STEVIE SMITH
Howards End, E. M. FORSTER
Miss Lonelyhearts, NATHANEAL WEST
Layabout, CHRISTOPHER LOGUE
The Awakening, KATE CHOPIN
Swann's Way, MARCEL PROUST
If the Nightflights, CHRISTOPHER LOGUE
Clarissa, SAMUEL RICHARDSON
Memoirs of a Fox-Hunting Man, SIEGFRIED SASSOON
The Waterfall, MARGARET DRABBLE
Confessions, JEAN JACQUES ROUSSEAU
Child's Poem, ANON

JOYCE GRENFELL

1970

The telephone rang. 'We must invite Noël to tea,' said one woman to another, summoning in the mind a social landscape of old-world courtesy and cucumber sandwiches. 'The poor dear hasn't been well.' Even today we are in no doubt that 'Noël' could only have been Noël Coward. The woman thus telephoned was Joyce Grenfell, the caller the Queen Mother. I only met Joyce Grenfell once, in a studio in the late 1960s. She told me of the 'phone call, and the tea that followed it, not to name drop – the thought would never have occurred to her – but to express her pleasure in the warmth of the Queen Mother's personality and the way in which she had included her as co-host of the occasion. They must have made a

glittering trio and to use the words 'common touch' in that context may
appear rather strange, but certainly the two women must have had it. I
have never in my rather neurotic occupation met anyone who had so little
sense of self and so much enjoyment of life and of other people, whoever
they may be, as Joyce Grenfell displayed during the few hours I spent in
her company.

I've taken the title 'With Great Pleasure' seriously. For me it
means the lifting of the heart in amusement or nourishment – a
kind of recognition of something that may be half forgotten or not
yet fully acknowledged; there is more to be discovered in the
book or poem that I go back to again and again.

I've deliberately left out the great names. The field is too wide
and the choice too difficult (Shakespeare, for instance!), so I've
made my selection a miniature one – smaller stars, but they go on
giving me an increasing illumination and *pleasure.*

A few years ago I met a Brown Franciscan brother in the
unlikely setting of the Picnic Races in a remote corner of Queens-
land in Australia who told me the best way to explain to people
what redemption means is to get them to read Frances Hodgson
Burnett's *The Secret Garden.*

It had never occurred to me. I've read the book over and over
again since I first had it, aged nine I think. It's got all the
ingredients for a good story and I still enjoy it. I've just read it
again. It has a sad beginning, mystery, cries in the night – and a
happy ending grown out of the emancipation and development
of the two central characters, Mary Lennox and her cousin Colin,
both about ten years old. Our heroine is a scraggy, spoilt,
unattractive orphan who comes from India to live with an anti-
social, unhappy, widowed uncle in his huge gloomy house in
Yorkshire on the edge of the moor. Mary learns that there is a
hidden 'secret garden' lost within the vast acres of the place.
Forlornly skipping down one of the many long paths, she comes
across a robin who apparently leads her to find an old key stuck in
a clod of newly-turned earth in a flower bed.

The Secret Garden
FRANCES HODGSON BURNETT

'You showed me where the key was yesterday,' she said. 'You ought to show me the door to-day; but I don't believe you know!' Mary had stepped close to the robin, and suddenly the gust of wind swung aside some loose ivy trails, and more suddenly still she jumped towards it and caught it in her hand. This she did because she had seen something under it – a round knob which had been covered by the leaves hanging over it. It was the knob of a door.

Mary's heart began to thump and her hands to shake a little in her delight and excitement. The robin kept singing and twittering away and tilting his head on one side, as if he were as excited as she was. What was this under her hands which was square and made of iron and which her fingers found a hole in?

It was the lock of the door which had been closed ten years, and she put her hand in her pocket, drew out the key, and found it fitted the keyhole. She put the key in and turned it. It took two hands to do it, but it did turn.

And then she took a long breath and looked behind her up the long walk to see if anyone was coming. No one was coming. She held back the swinging curtain of ivy and pushed back the door which opened slowly – slowly.

Then she slipped through it, and shut it behind her, and stood with her back against it, looking about her and breathing quite fast with excitement, and wonder, and delight. She was standing *inside* the secret garden.

Nannies, as they once were, played a very big part in the lives of those lucky enough to have been looked after by a good one. Nannies were reassuring, comfortable, kind, cosy and loving, *and always there*. At least mine was. Nannies had a special language, jokes worn thin with over use: 'hurry up now, you're all behind like a cow's tail' – 'come along now, up the stairs to Bedfordshire' – 'don't care was made to care'.

I had the best of all possible worlds, a mother whom I saw constantly (small house, that kind of mother) and a nanny for the in-between times whom we loved.

Priscilla Napier, who wrote *A Late Beginner*, has a wonderful ear for Nanny talk and an accurate eye for childish responses to it.

A Late Beginner
PRISCILLA NAPIER

Religion was dangerous ground with Nanny. One could not, as with one's parents, say anything, any time. Nanny's lips had a way of folding up, forbiddingly. The first time I heard the word Alleluia I was so enchanted with it that I spent ten minutes leaping up and down on the armchair in the far corner of the drawing-room loudly pronouncing it.

'Don't do that,' Nanny said, when she found me. Her voice had an edge.

'Alleluia!' I said, leaping higher. The springs sent one up and up, the sensation was glorious. Alleluia! Alleluia! Alleluia! It was highly enjoyable; I wanted never to stop.

'I said don't do that', Nanny said again, more sharply. 'You'll break the springs.' But one could tell it wasn't that she minded.

'Alleluia! Alleluia!' I said, boring of it very slightly but drawing her on. 'All-el-uia-a-a!'

'That's a holy word,' Nanny said, 'Not to be bandied about in play. I would think you'd know better.' She took me by the arm quite brusquely and led me off to have my face washed although we both knew it was perfectly clean.

I found this love poem in Walter de la Mare's anthology called *Love*. It's a wonderful collection and it has a long introduction that makes the whole book one to go back and back to. This poem is by Sylvia Lind – I see it as set in East Anglia in August sixty or seventy years ago.

The Happy Hour
SYLVIA LIND

H.L.A.L.; with penknife deep embedded,
   He carved the letters on the ancient stile.
Harry and Alice, rural lovers wedded,
   Stayed and were happy here a little while.

Along the dykes they walked, while the sun wested,

In the warm summer evening, and so it was
That Harry stood and carved, while Alice rested,
    Amid the knapweed and the tall bleached grass.

Blue shone the tide, the swallows skimmed and darted,
    White gulls passed slowly, redshanks made their cry;
The wheat was newly cut, the beans were carted,
    And haystacks golden-rooved against the sky.

Pale gold the oaten stocks above the clover,
    Too still the air to lift the thistledown,
Sometimes a curlew cried, sometimes a plover,
    And evening fullness grew, and the sun shone,

And stretched long shadows on the yellow stubble;
    While Harry set his oriflamme to prove
That, in a world called sad and full of trouble,
    Two people once were happy, being in love.

I have always loved visual detail – the detail of a flower, the hair-line design in a white violet petal, a snail's trail, a feather, a shell, indeed a grain of sand – and for the same reason as Blake – to see all heaven in.

I'm drawn to the sense of leisure, time to embroider, time to sit or stand and stare that seems to have operated in the Victorian and Edwardian eras. That is why for my first love poem I have chosen one by Dante Gabriel Rossetti – I've deliberately gone for *contented* love poems rather than anguished ones. I like a little agony here and there, but I'm after a calmer scene now.

Your Hands Lie Open
DANTE GABRIEL ROSSETTI

Your hands lie open in the long fresh grass, –
The finger-points look through like rosy blooms:
Your eyes smile peace. The pasture gleams and glooms
'Neath billowing skies that scatter and amass.
All round our nest, far as the eye can pass,
Are golden Kingcup-fields with silver edge
Where the cow-parsley skirts the hawthorn-hedge.
'Tis visible silence, still as the hour-glass.

Deep in the sun-searched growths the dragon-fly
Hangs like a blue thread loosened from the sky: –
So this winged hour is dropped to us from above.
Oh! clasp we to our hearts, for deathless dower,
This close-companioned inarticulate hour
When twofold silence was the song of love.

I have included a little anguish, and it too is both a portrait of an
era and a poem about love.

The Gifts Returned
WALTER SAVAGE LANDOR

'You must give back' her mother said
to a poor sobbing little maid,
'All the young man has given you,
Hard as it may now seem to do.'
''Tis done already, mother dear'
Said the sweet girl, 'So never fear.'
(M) 'Are you quite certain? Come, recount.
(There was not much) the whole amount.'
(G) The locket; the kid gloves.
(M) Go on.
(G) Of the kid gloves I found but one.
(M) Never mind that. What else? Proceed.
You gave back all his trash?
(G) Indeed.
(M) And was there nothing you would save?
(G) Everything I could give I gave.
(M) To the last tittle?
(G) Even to that.
(M) Freely?
(G) My heart went pit-a-pat
At giving up . . . ah me, ah me
I cry so I can hardly see. . . .
All the fond looks and words that passed
And all the kisses, to the last.

Reader: Cecil Day Lewis

Full Selection:
Autobiography, ENID BAGNOLD
The Secret Garden, FRANCES HODGSON BURNETT
A Late Beginner, PRISCILLA NAPIER
Who Goes There?, CECIL DAY LEWIS
In Memory of Basil Marquis of Dufferin and Ava, JOHN BETJEMAN
Words Come Best From Those Least Given to Speech, DORIS PEEL
Spring Song, VIRGINIA GRAHAM
Emma, JANE AUSTEN
The Happy Hour, SYLVIA LIND
Your Hands Lie Open, DANTE GABRIEL ROSSETTI
The Gifts Returned, WALTER SAVAGE LANDOR
Persuasion, JANE AUSTEN
A South African Childhood, VICTOR STIEBEL
A Hard Frost, CECIL DAY LEWIS
The Great Sneeze, PATRICK CAMPBELL
The Gospel According to John, THE NEW ENGLISH BIBLE
The Second Book of Kings, AUTHORISED VERSION

JO GRIMOND

1978

When, at an age too early to vote, I used to watch with my parents the party political broadcasts, Jo Grimond was always the man who talked the most sense and whose party gathered the least votes. No doubt the one was the reason for the other. He was also Liberal Member of Parliament for Orkney, a place which seemed strangely romantic and far away to one born and bred south of Watford. Certainly it exerts a powerful influence on those who left it to seek fame and fortune elsewhere. For such a tiny island it seems also to have bred a disproportionate number of fine writers, many of whom stayed put.

I was born in St Andrews in 1913 and St Andrews in those days was rather like Robert Louis Stevenson's Edinburgh. We too had a light outside our house and Larry the Lamplighter came to light it every evening. But it is Stevenson's *Windy Nights* which reminds me most of my childhood.

Windy Nights
ROBERT LOUIS STEVENSON

Whenever the moon and stars are set,
 Whenever the wind is high,
All night long in the dark and wet,
 A man goes riding by.
Late in the night when the fires are out,
 Why does he gallop and gallop about?

Whenever the trees are crying aloud,
 And ships are tossed at sea,
By, on the highway, low and loud,
 By at the gallop goes he.
By at the gallop he goes, and then
By he comes back at the gallop again.

From early days at school I was made to learn poetry by heart; I think it's a very excellent idea and especially if you're allowed to choose it yourself, as I was later on. I've always rather liked those didactic, well-turned, eighteenth-century writers like Gray and Burke, but in particular let's have a bit of Goldsmith on the village schoolmaster.

The Deserted Village
OLIVER GOLDSMITH

Beside yon straggling fence that skirts the way,
With blossom'd furze unprofitably gay,
There, in his noisy mansion, skill'd to rule,

The village master taught his little school;
A man severe he was, and stern to view;
I knew him well, and every truant knew;
Well had the boding tremblers learn'd to trace
The day's disasters in his morning face;
Full well they laugh'd, with counterfeited glee,
At all his jokes, for many a joke had he;
Full well the busy whisper, circling round,
Convey'd the dismal tidings when he frown'd;
Yet he was kind; or if severe in aught,
The love he bore to learning was in fault;
The village all declar'd how much he knew;
'Twas certain he could write, and cypher too;
Lands he could measure, terms and tides presage,
And e'en the story ran that he could gauge.
In arguing too, the parson own'd his skill,
For e'en though vanquish'd, he could argue still;
While words of learned length and thund'ring sound
Amazed the gazing rustics rang'd around,
And still they gaz'd, and still the wonder grew,
That one small head could carry all he knew.

As I'm a politician I think we must have a piece of rhetoric. The bit I've chosen is a well known speech by that old rogue Lord Palmerston. Palmerston had behaved in a fairly monstrous manner to the Greeks in defence of a very shady character called Don Pacifico who was in fact a Portuguese, but had acquired British citizenship, and a vote of censure was passed in the House of Lords and a vote of censure was put down in the House of Commons and it was expected to be passed too. However Old Pam turned up in the middle of the night and spoke for four and a half hours till daybreak and he carried the day quite easily.

Don Pacifico Debate
LORD PALMERSTON

We have shown that liberty is compatible with order; that individual freedom is reconcilable with obedience to the law. We have shown the example of a nation, in which every class of society accepts with cheerfulness the lot which Providence has assigned to it; while at the same time every individual of each class is constantly striving to raise himself in the social scale – not by injustice and wrong, not by violence and illegality – but by persevering good conduct, and by the steady and energetic exertion of the moral and intellectual faculties with which his Creator has endowed him. To govern such a people as this is indeed an object worthy of the ambition of the noblest man who lives in the land; and therefore, I find no fault with those who may think any opportunity a fair one, for endeavouring to place themselves in so distinguished and honourable a position. But I contend that we have not in our foreign policy done anything to forfeit the confidence of the country. . . . I therefore fearlessly challenge the verdict which this House, as representing a political, a commercial, a constitutional country, is to give on the question now brought before it; whether the principles on which the foreign policy of Her Majesty's Government has been conducted, and the sense of duty which has led us to think ourselves bound to afford protection to our fellow subjects abroad, are proper and fitting guides for those who are charged with the government of England; and whether, as the Roman in days of old, held himself free from indignity, when we could say 'Civis Romanus sum' so also a British subject, in whatever land he may be, shall feel confident that the watchful eye and the strong arm of England will protect him against injustice and wrong.

Palmerston was a remarkable old man; when he was over seventy and Prime Minister he is alleged to have seduced a girl at an official government reception. The Tories had the very greatest difficulty in preventing her outraged husband from taking action against him, because, as they rightly guessed, had he done so he would have won the forthcoming General Election by an even bigger majority than in fact he achieved. Now, I'm not a great reader of historical letters – I think letters should be rather tuned to the matter in hand, they should be quick comments on what is going on at the time. I don't think they should be written for posterity, but I rather like this letter written about Lord John Russell who was a contemporary and ally of Palmerston's, two terrible old men who terrified Queen Victoria and the Prince Consort.

Letter From Sydney Smith About Lord John Russell

There is not a better man in England than Lord John Russell; but his worst failure is that he is utterly ignorant of all moral fear; there is nothing he would not undertake. I believe he would perform the operation for the stone – build St Peter's – or assume (with or without ten minutes notice) the command of the Channel Fleet; and no one would discover by his manner that the patient had died – the Church tumbled down – and the Channel Fleet had been knocked to atoms. . . . Another peculiarity of the Russells is that they never alter their opinions; they are an excellent race, but they must be trepanned before they can be convinced.

Sydney Smith, believe it or not, was a clergyman and he made a lot of celebrated remarks. One of the best, I think, was about the Bishop of Exeter, about whom he said: 'Of course I must believe in the Apostolic Succession. How else can one account for the descent of the Bishop of Exeter from Judas Iscariot?'

Another letter I rather like is from the Duke of Wellington. The Duke was walking in the park one day when he met a boy who was crying. The Duke asked him why he was crying, to which the boy replied 'I have to go back to school tomorrow and my parents have told me I must get rid of my pet toad.'

'Give me your toad,' said the Duke, 'and I will look after it.'

So the boy went back to school and forgot all about his toad. A year later he received the following letter from the Duke of Wellington:

Field Marshal the Duke of Wellington presents his compliments to Mr So and So and requests that at his convenience he will be so good as to call and collect his toad.

Winter in Orkney is usually a time of wet and wind rather than snow and ice, in fact we tend to get our snow in the spring and 'The Lady of Shallott' may seem rather an odd choice to commemorate winter, but to me it does conjure up winter days.

The Lady of Shallott, Part IV
ALFRED LORD TENNYSON

In the stormy east-wind straining,
The pale yellow woods were waning,
The broad stream in his banks complaining,
Heavily the low sky raining
    Over tower'd Camelot;
Down she came and found a boat
Beneath a willow left afloat,
And round about the prow she wrote
    The Lady of Shallott.

And down the river's dim expanse –
Like some bold seer in a trance,
Seeing all his own mischance –
With a glassy countenance
    Did she look to Camelot.
And at the closing of the day
She loosed the chain, and down she lay;
The broad stream bore her far away,
    The Lady of Shallott.

Lying, robed in snowy white
That loosely flew to left and right –
The leaves upon her falling light –
Thro' the noises of the night
    She floated down to Camelot.
And as the boat-head wound along
The willowy hills and fields among,
They heard her singing her last song,
    The Lady of Shallott.

– Heard a carol, mournful, holy,
Chanted loudly, chanted lowly,
Till her blood was frozen slowly,
And her eyes were darken'd wholly,
    Turn'd to tower'd Camelot;
For ere she reach'd upon the tide
The first house by the water-side,

Singing in her song she died,
    The Lady of Shallott.

Under tower and balcony,
By garden-wall and gallery,
A gleaming shape she floated by,
Dead-pale between the houses high,
    Silent into Camelot.
Out upon the wharfs they came,
Knight and burgher, lord and dame,
And round the prow they read her name,
    The Lady of Shallott.

Who is this? and what is here?
And in the lighted palace near
Died the sound of royal cheer;
And they cross'd themselves for fear,
    All the knights at Camelot:
But Lancelot mused a little space;
He said, 'She has a lovely face;
God in his mercy lend her grace,
    The Lady of Shallott.'

Let us end on a cheerful and rather eccentric note – 'The Owl and
the Pussy-Cat' by Edward Lear, who must have been one of the
nicest men who ever lived.

The Owl and the Pussy-Cat
EDWARD LEAR

The Owl and the Pussy-Cat went to sea
    In a beautiful pea-green boat,
They took some honey, and plenty of money,
    Wrapped up in a five-pound note.
The Owl looked up to the stars above,
    And sang to a small guitar,
'O lovely Pussy! O Pussy, my love,
    What a beautiful Pussy you are,
        You are,
        You are,
What a beautiful Pussy you are!'

Pussy said to the Owl, 'You elegant fowl!
How charmingly sweet you sing!
O let us be married! too long we have tarried:
But what shall we do for a ring?'
They sailed away, for a year and a day,
To the land where the Bong-tree grows
And there in a wood a Piggy-wig stood
With a ring at the end of his nose,
His nose,
His nose,
With a ring at the end of his nose.

'Dear Pig, are you willing to sell for one shilling
Your ring?' Said the Piggy, 'I will.'
So they took it away, and were married next day
By the Turkey who lives on the hill.
They dined on mince, and slices of quince,
Which they ate with a runcible spoon;
And hand in hand, on the edge of the sand,
They danced by the light of the moon,
The moon,
The moon,
They danced by the light of the moon.

Readers: Alan Dobie, Diana Olsson, Howie Firth

Full Selection:
Genesis, V: 1–27, THE BIBLE
The Origin of Species, CHARLES DARWIN
Windy Nights, ROBERT LOUIS STEVENSON
Childhood, EDWIN MUIR
Matilda, Who Told Lies and Was Burned to Death, HILAIRE BELLOC
Stiff Upper Lip, Jeeves, P. G. WODEHOUSE
The Deserted Village, OLIVER GOLDSMITH
Sailing to Byzantium, W. B. YEATS
Don Pacifico Debate, LORD PALMERSTON
A Letter, SYDNEY SMITH
A Letter, DUKE OF WELLINGTON

A Shropshire Lad, A. E. HOUSMAN
The Mower to the Slow-Worms, ANDREW MARVELL
In Memoriam, ALFRED LORD TENNYSON
The Lady of Shallott, Part IV ALFRED LORD TENNYSON
Da Sang O Da Papa Men, ANON
Orkney Crofter, ROBERT RENDALL
Hamnavoe, GEORGE MACKAY BROWN
The Sun Rising, JOHN DONNE
The Owl and the Pussy-Cat, EDWARD LEAR

EDWARD HEATH

1980

*There are probably few modern prime ministers who, whatever their
virtues and shortcomings in public life, have had such diverse interests
outside politics as Edward Heath. One cannot be certain, of course, but
it is somehow difficult to imagine Margaret Thatcher, as she commands
the duties of high office, seeking the consolations of great music or fine
literature. Heath, on the other hand, as well as being a keen reader, enjoys
making music and sailing, gregarious occupations both. Nevertheless, he
remains essentially a private man and little that is personal was revealed
during the recording. He does, however, and this is perhaps another way
in which he differs from our current PM, display a well-developed sense
of humour.*

I went in to the City to be trained as a merchant banker. On the
day I arrived there I was taken by one of the senior members into
his room and he pointed, just above his fireplace, to a piece of
poetry (almost) which was written there; and he said, 'Young

man, just read this.' And what I read was this piece written in the sixteenth century.

The Heir of Adventure
NICOLAS BRETON

A worthy Merchant is the Heir of Adventure, whose hopes hang much upon the winds.

Upon a Wooden horse he rides through the World, and in a Merry gale makes a path through the seas.

He is a discoverer of countries and a finder-out of commodities, resolute in his attempts and royal in his Expenses.

He is the life of traffic and the Maintenance of trade, the Sailors' Master and the Soldiers' friend.

He is the Exercise of the Exchange, the honour of Credit, the observation of time, and the understanding of thrift.

His Study is Number, his Care his accounts, his Comfort his Conscience, and his Wealth his good Name.

He fears not Scylla and sails close by Charybdis, and having beaten out a Storm rides at rest in a harbour.

By his sea gain he makes his land purchase, and by the Knowledge of trade finds the Key of his treasure.

Out of his travels he makes his discourses, and from his Eye-observations brings the Model of Architecture.

He plants the Earth with foreign fruits, and knows at home what is good abroad.

He is Neat in apparel, Modest in demeanor, dainty in diet, and Civil in his Carriage.

In sum, he is the pillar of a City, the Enricher of a Country, the furnisher of a Court, and the Worthy Servant of a King.

'That,' he said, 'should guide you all your life in business.' I very soon went into politics.

And the next piece is taken from one of the greatest of our political writers, Edmund Burke. It's an essay, written in 1770, with a title which is perhaps not entirely unusual.

Thoughts on the Cause of the Present Discontents, 1770
EDMUND BURKE

I remember an old scholastic aphorism, which says, 'that the man who lives wholly detached from others must be either an angel or a devil'. When I see in any of these detached gentlemen of our times the angelic purity, power, and beneficence, I shall admit them to be angels. In the meantime we are born only to be men. We shall do enough if we form ourselves to be good ones. It is therefore our business carefully to cultivate in our minds, to rear to the most perfect vigour and maturity, every sort of generous and honest feeling, that belongs to our nature. To bring the dispositions that are lovely in private life into the service and conduct of the commonwealth; so to be patriots as not to forget we are gentlemen. To cultivate friendships, and to incur enmities. To have both strong, but both selected; in the one, to be placable; in the other immovable. To model our principles to our duties and our situation. To be fully persuaded that all virtue which is impracticable is spurious; and rather to run the risk of falling into faults in a course which leads us to act with effect and energy, than to loiter out our days without blame and without use. Public life is a situation of power and energy; he trespasses against his duty who sleeps upon his watch, as well as he that goes over to the enemy.

George Borrow is a man who is not very often read today. He wrote at the beginning of the nineteenth century. *Lavengro*, the story of a scholar, a gypsy and a priest, appealed to me when I first read it as a young boy. I chose the next piece from it, because although to begin with it deals with death, in the second part it shows the real joy of living and the desire of people to live.

Lavengro
GEORGE BORROW

I now wandered along the heath till I came to a place where, beside a thick furze, sat a man, his eyes fixed intently on the red ball of the setting sun.

'That's not you, Jasper?'
'Indeed, brother!'

'I've not seen you for years.'
'How should you, brother?'
'What brings you here?'
'The fight, brother.'
'Where are the tents?'
'On the old spot, brother.'
'Any news since we parted?'
'Two deaths, brother.'
'Who are dead, Jasper?'
'Father and mother, brother.'
'Where did they die?'
'Where they were sent, brother.'
'And Mrs. Herne?'
'She's alive, brother.'
'Where is she now?'
'In Yorkshire, brother.'
'What is your opinion of death, Mr. Petulengro?' said I, as I sat down beside him.

'My opinion of death, brother, is much the same as that in the old song of Pharaoh, which I have heard my grandam sing: –

"Cana marel o manus chivios andé puv,
Ta rovel pa leste o chavo ta romi".

When a man dies he is cast into the earth, and his wife and child sorrow over him. If he has neither wife nor child, then his father and mother, I suppose; and if he is quite alone in the world, why, then, he is cast into the earth, and there is the end of the matter.'
'And do you think that is the end of man?'
'There's an end of him, brother, more's the pity.'
'Why do you say so?'
'Life is sweet, brother.'
'Do you think so?'
'Think so! There's night and day, brother, both sweet things; sun, moon and stars, brother, all sweet things; there's likewise a wind on the heath. Life is very sweet, brother; who would wish to die?'
'I would wish to die. . . .'
'You talk like a Gorgio – which is the same as talking like a fool.

Were you a Rommany Chal, you would talk wiser. Wish to die, indeed! A Rommany Chal would wish to live for ever!'
   'In sickness, Jasper?'
   'There's the sun and stars, brother.'
   'In blindness, Jasper?'
   'There's the wind on the heath, brother; if I could only feel that, I would gladly live for ever. Dosta, we'll now go to the tents and put on the gloves; and I'll try to make you feel what a sweet thing it is to be alive, brother!'

Naturally you will be expecting something from me about the sea. I have chosen Walt Whitman's 'A Song for All Seas, All Ships'. These were the words which Ralph Vaughan Williams used for the Sea Symphony, his first major work:

A Song for All Seas, All Ships
WALT WHITMAN

Behold, the sea itself,
And on its limitless, heaving breast, the ships;
See, where their white sails, bellying in the wind, speckle the
   green and blue,
See, the steamers coming and going, steaming in or out of port,
See, dusky and undulating, the long pennants of smoke.
Behold, the sea itself,
And on its limitless, heaving breast, the ships.

Verse now of a different kind: the vigour and rhythm of Kipling's 'Mine Sweepers', which for me has a particular attraction because it is about the Foreland and about the Channel. So much of my life has been spent near the Foreland and sailing in the Channel.

Mine Sweepers
RUDYARD KIPLING

Dawn off the Foreland – the young flood making
   Jumbled and short and steep –
Black in the hollows and bright where it's breaking –
   Awkward water to sweep.
   'Mines reported in the fairway,
   'Warn all traffic and detain.

'Sent up Unity, Claribel, Assyrian, Stormcock,
   and Golden Gain.'

Noon off the Foreland – the first ebb making
   Lumpy and strong in the bight.
Boom after boom, and the golf-hut shaking
   And the jackdaws wild with fright!
   'Mines located in the fairway,
   'Boats now working up the chain,
'Sweepers – Unity, Claribel, Assyrian, Stormcock,
   and Golden Gain.'

Dusk off the Foreland – the last light going
   And the traffic crowding through,
And five damned trawlers with their syreens blowing
   Heading the whole review!
   'Sweep completed in the fairway.
   'No more mines remain.
'Sent back Unity, Claribel, Assyrian, Stormcock,
   and Golden Gain.'

I have chosen items of prose and poetry which have not only given me pleasure, but also reflect the various interests which I have in life. It's quite natural, I think, to include the Bible, because it has great influence on one in one's early life – it certainly did on me. But much, much more than that, it contains some of the most beautiful English prose, and indeed some would say poetry, in the psalms. I've chosen a piece from Ecclesiastes. I did so because it emphasizes the importance of time in life – the importance of timing. It is true of everything which one does, and it's certainly true in politics.

Ecclesiastes, Chapter 3, Verses 1–15

To every thing there is a season, and a time to every purpose
   under the heaven:
A time to be born, and a time to die; a time to plant, and a time
   to pluck up that which is planted;
A time to kill, and a time to heal; a time to break down and a
   time to build up;

A time to weep, and a time to laugh; a time to mourn, and a time
to dance;

A time to cast away stones, and a time to gather stones together;
a time to embrace, and a time to refrain from embracing;

A time to get and a time to lose; a time to keep, and a time to cast
away;

A time to rend, and a time to sew; a time to keep silence, and a
time to speak;

A time to love, and a time to hate; a time of war, and a time of
peace. What profit hath he that worketh in that wherein he
laboureth?

I have seen the travail, which God hath given to the sons of men
to be exercised in it.

He hath made every thing beautiful in his time: also he hath set
the world in their heart, so that no man can find out the work
that God maketh from the beginning to the end.

I know that there is no good in them, but for a man to rejoice,
and to do good in his life.

And also that every man should eat and drink, and enjoy the
good of all his labour, it is the gift of God.

I know that, whatsoever God doeth, it shall be for ever: nothing
can be put to it, nor any thing taken from it: and God doeth it,
that men should fear before him.

That which hath been is now; and that which is to be hath
already been; and God requireth that which is past.

Readers: Norman Rodway, Michael Williams

Full Selection:
The Heir of Adventure, NICOLAS BRETON
Thoughts on the Cause of the Present Discontents, EDMUND BURKE
On England, STANLEY BALDWIN
Memoirs of a Fox-Hunting Man, SIEGFRIED SASSOON
Collect for 4th Sunday after Easter, THE PRAYER BOOK
A Short History of the English People, JOHN RICHARD GREEN
Lavengro, GEORGE BORROW
Sonnet for the Madonna of the Cherries, LORD WAVELL
A Song for All Seas, All Ships, WALT WHITMAN

BRIAN JOHNSTON

1985

'Oh, good Lord, I'm not a great reader, Dick Francis, that sort of thing,' was Brian Johnston's first response on being asked if he would like to present an edition of 'With Great Pleasure'. In the event he seemed to have rather underplayed himself, but even if he hadn't, it was hardly the point. As a cricket commentator and broadcaster he has been a friendly and entertaining presence on radio and television for many years. He is also, apparently, one of the most popular after-dinner speakers in the country. After a hilarious evening spent in his company I can well believe it. A sentimental man, easily moved to tears, he was visibly moved at the reading from Oscar Wilde's 'The Selfish Giant'.

I've been lucky all my life. I had marvellous parents, brothers and sisters and I'm now very luckily possessed of a lovely wife and a family of five. And like me when I was a small boy, I think they loved *Alice in Wonderland* and *Alice Through the Looking Glass*: it was like entering another world. I haven't chosen the Mad Hatter's tea party, although it makes me laugh, but instead here is Tweedledee telling Alice about the Walrus and the Carpenter – I think it is the first time I ever remember feeling really sorry for anyone, those poor little oysters being conned by two confidence tricksters.

The Walrus and the Carpenter
LEWIS CARROLL

The sun was shining on the sea,
  Shining with all his might:
He did his very best to make
  The billows smooth and bright –
And this was odd, because it was
  The middle of the night.

The moon was shining sulkily,
  Because she thought the sun
Had got no business to be there
  After the day was done –
'It's very rude of him,' she said
  'To come and spoil the fun!'

The sea was wet as wet could be,
  The sands were dry as dry.
You could not see a cloud, because
  No cloud was in the sky:
No birds were flying overhead –
  There were no birds to fly.

The Walrus and the Carpenter
  Were walking close at hand:
They wept like anything to see
  Such quantities of sand:
'If this were only cleared away,'
  They said, 'it would be grand!'

'If seven maids with seven mops
  Swept it for half a year,
Do you suppose,' the Walrus said,

'That they could get it clear?'
'I doubt it,' said the Carpenter,
  And shed a bitter tear.

'O Oysters, come and walk with us!'
  The Walrus did beseech.
'A pleasant walk, a pleasant talk,
  Along the briny beach:
We cannot do with more than four,
  To give a hand to each.'

The eldest Oyster looked at him,
  But never a word he said:
The eldest Oyster winked his eye,
  And shook his heavy head –
Meaning to say he did not choose
  To leave the oyster-bed.

But four young Oysters hurried up,
  All eager for the treat:
Their coats were brushed, their faces washed,
  Their shoes were clean and neat –
And this was odd, because, you know,
  They hadn't any feet.

Four other Oysters followed them,
  And yet another four;
And thick and fast they came at last,
  And more, and more, and more –
All hopping through the frothy waves,
  And scrambling to the shore.

The Walrus and the Carpenter
  Walked on a mile or so,
And then they rested on a rock
  Conveniently low:
And all the little Oysters stood
  And waited in a row.

'The time has come,' the Walrus said,
  'To talk of many things:
Of shoes – and ships – and sealing wax –

Of cabbages – and kings –
And why the sea is boiling hot –
   And whether pigs have wings.'

'But wait a bit,' the Oysters cried,
   'Before we have our chat;
For some of us are out of breath,
   And all of us are fat.'
'No hurry!' said the Carpenter.
   They thanked him much for that.

'A loaf of bread,' the Walrus said,
   'Is what we chiefly need:
Pepper and vinegar besides
   Are very good indeed –
Now if you're ready, Oysters dear,
   We can begin to feed.'

'But not on us!' the Oysters cried,
   Turning a little blue.
'After such kindness, that would be
   A dismal thing to do!'
'The night is fine,' the Walrus said.
   'Do you admire the view?

'It was so kind of you to come!
   And you are very nice!'
The Carpenter said nothing but
   'Cut us another slice.
I wish you were not quite so deaf –
   I've had to ask you twice!'

'It seems a shame,' the Walrus said,
   'To play them such a trick.
After we've brought them out so far,
   And made them trot so quick!'
The Carpenter said nothing but
   'The butter's spread too thick!'

'I weep for you,' the Walrus said:
   'I deeply sympathize.'
With sobs and tears he sorted out

Those of the largest size,
Holding his pocket-handkerchief
Before his streaming eyes.

'O Oysters,' said the Carpenter,
'You've had a pleasant run!
Shall we be trotting home again?'
But answer came there none –
And this was scarcely odd, because
They'd eaten every one!

As I grew up, I think like any boy, I was very keen on comics –
things like *The Little Red Mag* or *Tiger Tim's Weekly* – but by the time
I was eight I'd already begun to read Conan Doyle's stories of
Sherlock Holmes. We were living in Hertfordshire at the time, in
the depths of the country, and our garden backed on to a big field;
as I read *The Hound of the Baskervilles* I imagined that this field was
Dartmoor which was haunted by this terrifying hound. It had
already killed Sir Hugo and Sir Charles Baskerville, whose family
had lived at Baskerville Hall for several centuries. And now the
present holder of the title, Sir Henry Baskerville, was persuaded
by Sherlock Holmes to act as bait in order to catch the hound, so
here we have Sherlock Holmes and Doctor Watson waiting with
Inspector Lestrade in a swirling fog out on the moor. It still
terrifies me.

The Hound of the Baskervilles
SIR ARTHUR CONAN DOYLE

A sound of quick steps broke the silence of the moor. Crouching
among the stones, we stared intently at the silver-tipped bank in
front of us. The steps grew louder, and through the fog, as
through a curtain, there stepped the man whom we were await-
ing. He looked round him in surprise as he emerged into the
clear, starlit night. Then came swiftly along the path, passed close
to where we lay, and went on up the long slope behind us. As he
walked he glanced continually over either shoulder, like a man
who is ill at ease.

'Hist!' cried Holmes, and I heard the sharp click of a cocking
pistol. 'Look out! It's coming!'

There was a thin, crisp continuous patter from somewhere in the heart of that crawling bank. The cloud was within fifty yards of where we lay, and we glared at it, all three, uncertain what horror was about to break from the heart of it. I was at Holmes' elbow, and I glanced for an instant at his face. It was pale and exultant, his eyes shining brightly in the moonlight. But suddenly they started forward in a rigid, fixed stare, and his lips parted in amazement. At the same instant Lestrade gave a yell of terror and threw himself face downwards upon the ground. I sprang to my feet, my inert hand grasping my pistol, my mind paralysed by the dreadful shape which had sprung out upon us from the shadows of the fog.

A hound it was, an enormous coal-black hound, but not such a hound as mortal eyes have ever seen. Fire burst from its open mouth, its eyes glowed with a smouldering glare, its muzzle and hackles and dewlap were outlined in flickering flame. Never in the delirious dream of a disordered brain could anything more savage, more appalling, more hellish, be conceived than that dark form and savage face which broke upon us out of the wall of fog.

With long bounds the huge black creature was leaping down the track, following hard upon the footsteps of our friend. So paralysed were we by the apparition that we allowed him to pass before we had recovered our nerve. Then Holmes and I both fired together, and the creature gave a hideous howl, which showed that one at least had hit him. He did not pause, however, but bounded onwards. Far away on the path we saw Sir Henry looking back, his face white in the moonlight, his hands raised in horror, glaring helplessly at the frightful thing which was hunting him down.

But that cry of pain from the hound had blown all our fears to the winds. If he was vulnerable he was mortal, and if we could wound him we could kill him. Never have I seen a man run as Holmes ran that night. I am reckoned fleet of foot, but he outpaced me as much as I outpaced the little professional. . . .

In front of us as we flew up the track we heard scream after scream from Sir Henry and the deep roar of the hound. I was in time to see the beast spring upon its victim, hurl him to the ground and worry at his throat. But the next instant Holmes had emptied five barrels of his revolver into the creature's flank. With a last howl of agony and a vicious snap in the air it rolled upon its back, four feet pawing furiously, and then fell limp upon its side. I stooped, panting, and pressed my pistol to the dreadful, shimmering head, but it was useless to pull the trigger. The giant hound was dead.

Sir Henry lay insensible where he had fallen. We tore away his collar, and Holmes breathed a prayer of gratitude when we saw that there was no sign of a wound and that the rescue had been in time. Already our friend's eyelids shivered and he made a feeble effort to move. Lestrade thrust his brandy-flask between the baronet's teeth, and two frightened eyes were looking up at us.

'My God!' he whispered. 'What was it? What, in Heaven's name, was it?'

'It's dead, whatever it is,' said Holmes. 'We've laid the family ghost once and for ever.'

To end I've chosen a little masterpiece, a book which I keep by my bedside. I read it frequently: it's by Alan Miller and it's about a lovable old parson called Septimus. As a curate he'd once bowled a famous English cricketer called Ulysses, but his work as a parson in the slums had prevented him from playing any more cricket. The time is now 1948 and he's very ill with heart trouble, too ill to go and see the final test against Australia at the Oval, and he was very worried that England was going to be beaten again. On the night before the Test he went to bed early feeling ill and soon fell into a deep sleep and dreamt that he'd been selected to play for England as a mystery bowler.

Close of Play
ALAN MILLER

After a firm handshake and a confident smile from Ulysses, Septimus – closely behind his captain, and with Bedser at his side – went out with the rest of the team. When the welcoming applause had subsided, he heard the buzz that went round the ground as the spectators became aware of his plump little figure and bald head. But he didn't mind – not a bit! He knew somehow that he wasn't going to let Ulysses and the Old Country down.

Very soon Morris and Barnes were at the wicket. They looked

determined and formidable. He expected them to. After all they were great batsmen with wonderful records! He trotted down to his place in the field. The buzz was louder here, since he was only a few yards from the boundary. But he had worked for years in a London slum; he knew these kindly Cockneys. They wouldn't make fun of him! And if he did well, how they would take him to their hearts – as indeed they had done, for other reasons, years ago. No, he could hear no jeering. One wag shouted 'Good luck to you, Daddy!' But he liked that! He knew it was meant sincerely. He was tempted to turn and smile his thanks; but the game was about to begin.

Bedser bowled the first over – hefty, energetic stuff. It was a maiden; and the batsman left three tempting outswingers alone. Then came the great moment! He walked up to the wicket, and Yardley, smiling, handed him the ball. 'Good luck, old man!' he said – and dash it, the great big chap seemed a bit upset!

He gave his sweater to the umpire – a contemporary! He grinned. Did he sense what was coming? The buzzing in the crowd sank almost to silence. Doubtless the 'knowalls' were wondering how a man of his age could bowl fast – for there had been but one over with the new ball. The side knew where to field for him: they had been carefully instructed. Barnes, looking very aggressive, took his guard. He surveyed the scene and then prepared to face this new England bowler who, for some reason, had been exhumed from the past.

Septimus took but four or five short steps in his run-up. Over went his arm, and the wizardry of those long fingers began. His first ball – a very slow one – was on its way!

Barnes watched it carefully: he was taking no chances. It was well pitched up to him on the line of the off stump. He played forward, but misjudged its length. It was a leg-break – a tremendous break too! When the ball was caught at second slip, the crowd went mad; but the bat had gone nowhere near it. Barnes looked at the pitch and prodded it with his bat. Yardley, at mid-off, smiled broadly. The next ball was of a different length and a shade faster. Barnes was in two minds about it, but decided to step back and play a push shot. He was just in time. The ball kept very low. He managed to stop it with the bottom of his bat. It travelled a foot.

Septimus sent down a simple full-toss which Barnes promptly hit for six. Yardley looked inquiringly at the bowler. He got a wink in reply. The next was also a full-toss, but of a different kind. This one wasn't ground bait! Barnes went for it, but the ball did something curious in the air. It seemed to swing a lot and it changed its expected trajectory towards the end of its flight. Barnes 'failed to connect' – failed by quite a great deal! It fell about eighteen inches from the wicket, broke in smartly, and the leg stump went back. The crowd yelled – loudly and long – and Barnes, not looking very pleased, departed.

Well, Septimus continued to astonish the crowd. He bowled Bradman for a duck and took five for twenty and Australia had to follow on and they collapsed. And then with one wicket to fall Sam Loxton hit a skier down to Septimus at long leg. . . .

Up and up it went. Surely a grand six. Septimus watched it fascinated, then suddenly he realised that it might not carry the distance. By Jove, it might be a catch. Johosaphat, he'd show them he could do more than bowl. He set off at full speed along the boundary cheered frantically by the friendly crowd, madly cheered, as if he were a potential Derby winner. But alas it seemed that he would never get there in time, it looked like coming down a yard from the fence. At roughly six feet from where he judged it must fall, he made a violent effort. He might just manage it. He dived forward, at full length, his arms outstretched, his hands ready to grasp the ball. And fell flat on his face.

The next morning his wife found Septimus, lying on the bedroom floor, with his arm flung out as if he'd died trying to grasp something in his right hand. If only he could have lived a little longer, she said wistfully, it's sad to think he missed the last test. Missed the last test? Set your heart at rest dear lady, he didn't miss the last test, he won it.

Readers: Ian Carmichael, Julia Foster

Full Selection:
I Was There, PETER TINNISWOOD
The Walrus and the Carpenter, LEWIS CARROLL

The Hound of the Baskervilles, SIR ARTHUR CONAN DOYLE
The Road to Mandalay, BILLY BENNETT
England, Their England, A. G. MACDONNELL
The Selfish Giant, OSCAR WILDE
Onwards to Victory, SIR WINSTON CHURCHILL
The Max Miller Blue Book, MAX MILLER
Leave It to Jeeves, P. G. WODEHOUSE
Close of Play, ALAN MILLER

GEORGE MACBETH

1987

It has been my pleasure to know George MacBeth for many years, since the time when, as the BBC's poetry producer, he included a poem of mine in Radio 3's 'Poetry Now'. He is currently presenting 'Time for Verse' on Radio 4, which gives me the opportunity to produce him! I have always enjoyed his sly wit and sense of mischief: indelibly etched on my memory is seeing him, during a brief respite from a poetry-reading tour in the West Country, striding across muddy, windswept Dartmoor dressed for the city in pinstripe suit, polished shoes, and carrying a rolled umbrella. 'If you are properly dressed you can go anywhere,' he said. I don't know about that, but we all looked less than well turned out by the time we finally reached a friendly pub.

You can't be a Scotsman and not admire Sir Walter Scott. Scott always thought of himself as a poet and he was very proud that for several years, in his own words, he had 'had the palm' before the rise of his admired younger contemporary and friend Lord Byron. We don't enough enjoy Scott's magnificent ballads and narrative poems nowadays. They stand the test of time very well, they contain genuine feeling and they move with a real surge of rhythm.

Lochinvar
SIR WALTER SCOTT

O Young Lochinvar is come out of the west,
Through all the wide Border his steed was the best;
And save his good broadsword he weapons had none,
He rode all unarm'd and he rode all alone,
So faithful in love, and so dauntless in war,
There never was knight like the young Lochinvar.

He staid not for brake, and he stopp'd not for stone,
He swam the Eske river where ford there was none;
But ere he alighted at Netherby gate,
The bride had consented, the gallant came late:
For a laggard in love, and a dastard in war,
Was to wed the fair Ellen of brave Lochinvar.

So boldly he enter'd the Netherby Hall,
Among bride's-men, and kinsmen, and brothers and all:
Then spoke the bride's father, his hand on his sword,
(For the poor craven bridegroom said never a word),
'O come ye in peace here, or come ye in war,
Or to dance at our bridal, young Lord Lochinvar?'

The bride kiss'd the goblet: the knight took it up,
He quaff'd off the wine, and he threw down the cup.
She look'd down to blush, and she look'd up to sigh,
With a smile on her lips and a tear in her eye.
He took her soft hand, ere her mother could bar, –
'Now tread we a measure!' said Young Lochinvar.

One touch to her hand, and one word in her ear,
When they reach'd the hall-door, and the charger stood near;
So light to the croupe the fair lady he swung,
So light to the saddle before her he sprung!
'She is won! we are gone, over bank, bush, and scaur;
They'll have fleet steeds that follow,' quoth Young Lochinvar.

There was mounting 'mong Graemes of the Netherby clan;
Forsters, Fenwicks, and Musgraves, they rode and they ran:
There was racing and chasing on Cannobie Lee,
But the lost bride of Netherby ne'er did they see.
So daring in love, and so dauntless in war,
Have ye e'er heard of gallant like Young Lochinvar?

I'm sure Sir Walter would agree with me that you can't be a
Scotsman with my name and not admire Shakespeare – even if
the famous play with the unlucky title did persecute my childhood with endless jokes. What bloody man is this? and so on. So
to set the standard we all have to fight for, here we have the
bloody lady, so to call her, in full spate from Act One, Scene Five.

Macbeth
WILLIAM SHAKESPEARE

Inverness, MACBETH'S *Castle*
Enter Lady MACBETH, *reading a letter*

'They met me in the day of success; and I have learn'd by the
perfect'st report they have more in them than mortal knowledge.
When I burn'd in desire to question them further, they made
themselves air, into which they vanish'd. Whiles I stood rapt in
the wonder of it, came missives from the King, who all-hailed me
"Thane of Cawdor"; by which title, before, these weird sisters
saluted me, and referr'd me to the coming on of time with "Hail,
king that shalt be!" This have I thought good to deliver thee, my
dearest partner of greatness, that thou mightest not lose the dues
of rejoicing by being ignorant of what greatness is promis'd thee.
Lay it to thy heart, and farewell.'

Glamis thou art, and Cawdor; and shalt be
What thou art promised. Yet I do fear thy nature;
It is too full o' the milk of human kindness
To catch the nearest way. Thou wouldst be great;
Art not without ambition, but without
The illness should attend it; what thou wouldst highly,
That would thou holily; wouldst not play false,
And yet wouldst wrongly win; thou'dst have, great Glamis,
That which cries 'Thus thou must do, if thou have it';

And that which rather thou dost fear to do
Than wishest should be undone. Hie thee hither,
That I may pour my spirits in thine ear,
And chastise with the valour of my tongue
All that impedes thee from the golden round,
Which fate and metaphysical aid doth seem
To have thee crown'd withal. . . .

          Come, you spirits
That tend on mortal thoughts! unsex me here,
And fill me from the crown to the toe top full
Of direst cruelty; make thick my blood,
Stop up the access and passage to remorse,
That no compunctious visitings of nature
Shake my fell purpose, nor keep peace between
The effect and it! Come to my woman's breasts,
And take my milk for gall, you murdering ministers,
Wherever in your sightless substances
You wait on nature's mischief! Come, thick night,
And pall thee in the dunnest smoke of hell,
That my keen knife see not the wound it makes,
Nor heaven peep through the blanket of the dark
To cry 'Hold, hold!'

When I went up to Oxford in the early fifties the vogue in literary circles was very much for a kind of rigidly corseted metaphysical poem which owed a good deal more to William Empson than Andrew Marvell. But I did very quickly start to gulp down a delicious diet of minor Caroline lyricists like Suckling and Carew and one or two more far-flung classically minded writers like the formidable Dr Johnson. Here is his magisterial and moral elegy on the life of a friend who was a doctor.

Lines on the Death of Mr Levett
SAMUEL JOHNSON

Condemn'd to Hope's delusive mine,
  As on we toil from day to day,
By sudden blast or slow decline,
  Our social comforts drop away.

Well try'd through many a varying year,
   See LEVETT to the grave descend;
Officious, innocent, sincere,
   Of ev'ry friendless name the friend.

Yet still he fills Affection's eye,
   Obscurely wise, and coarsely kind,
Nor, letter'd arrogance, deny
   Thy praise to merit unrefin'd.

When fainting Nature call'd for aid,
   And hov'ring Death prepar'd the blow,
His vigorous remedy display'd
   The pow'r of art without the show.

In Misery's darkest caverns known,
   His ready help was ever nigh,
Where hopeless Anguish pours his groan,
   And lonely want retir'd to die.

No summons mock'd by chill delay,
   No petty gains disdain'd by pride;
The modest wants of ev'ry day
   The toil of ev'ry day supply'd.

His virtues walk'd their narrow round,
   Nor made a pause, nor left a void;
And sure th'Eternal Master found
   His single talent well employ'd.

The busy day, the peaceful night,
   Unfelt, uncounted, glided by;
His frame was firm, his powers were bright,
   Though now his eightieth year was nigh.

Then, with no throbs of fiery pain,
   No cold gradations of decay,
Death broke at once the vital chain,
   And freed his soul the nearest way.

Not many poets can achieve that sort of emotional intensity right
on the brink of prose. I kept the Levett poem in mind when I was

trying to write my own fledgling elegy for an elderly Sheffield cutler, who took me into his house when my mother died. But I couldn't live up to the Johnson standard. I couldn't live up to the Louis MacNeice one either when I joined the BBC in 1955 as a general trainee. But it was the fact of MacNeice being employed by the BBC that made me feel it would be an organization worth working for. I knew that he'd been able to write the best radio play ever – *The Dark Tower* – while employed by Features Department and I had a fantasy I could follow in his footsteps. But I ended up as a minor cultural functionary in Talks Department. Here, anyway, is MacNeice in another challenging vein, illustrating how a foreigner, an Ulsterman to boot, can catch the ironical swing and drive of the Scottish national instrument, as no one else has done.

Bagpipe Music
LOUIS MACNEICE

It's no go the merrygoround, it's no go the rickshaw,
All we want is a limousine and a ticket for the peepshow.
Their knickers are made of crêpe-de-chine, their shoes are made
  of python,
Their halls are lined with tiger rugs and their walls with heads of
  bison.

John MacDonald found a corpse, put it under the sofa,
Waited till it came to life and hit it with a poker,
Sold its eyes for souvenirs, sold its blood for whisky,
Kept its bones for dumb-bells to use when he was fifty.

It's no go the Yogi-Man, it's no go Blavatsky,
All we want is a bank balance and a bit of skirt in a taxi.

Annie MacDougall went to milk, caught her foot in the heather,
Woke to hear a dance record playing of Old Vienna.
It's no go your maidenheads, it's no go your culture,
All we want is a Dunlop tyre and the devil mend the puncture.

The Laird o' Phelps spent Hogmanay declaring he was sober,
Counted his feet to prove the fact and found he had one foot
  over.
Mrs Carmichael had her fifth, looked at the job with repulsion,

Said to the midwife 'Take it away; I'm through with
  over-production'.

It's no go the gossip column, it's no go the Ceilidh,
All we want is a mother's help and a sugar-stick for the baby.

Willie Murray cut his thumb, couldn't count the damage,
Took the hide of an Ayrshire cow and used it for a bandage.
His brother caught three hundred cran when the seas were
  lavish,
Threw the bleeders back in the sea and went upon the parish.

It's no go the Herring Board, it's no go the Bible,
All we want is a packet of fags when our hands are idle.

It's no go the picture palace, it's no go the stadium,
It's no go the country cot with a pot of pink geraniums,
It's no go the Government grants, it's no go the elections,
Sit on your arse for fifty years and hang your hat on a pension.

It's no go my honey love, it's no go my poppet;
Work your hands from day to day, the winds will blow the
  profit.
The glass is falling hour by hour, the glass will fall for ever,
But if you break the bloody glass you won't hold up the
  weather.

The vernacular line, the kind of low style that took over after the
death of Dylan Thomas, reaches a fine climax in the best of Adrian
Mitchell, the doyen of poetry performers on the hustings, and a
poet who once said that a poet should shake – when reading his
own work aloud – like an engine shakes. Well, I think there's
enough energy in the political Mitchell to need a belt across its
bonnet like an old Morgan.

'Tell Me Lies About Vietnam' galvanized a generation, and
then 'An Oxford Hysteria of English Poetry' set us all laughing all
the way to the voting booth. It's a genuinely hilarious whistle-
stop tour of the main landmarks in our great national heritage,
those dusty volumes lining the library shelves and waiting to
burst into flame at the spark of a new imagination. Well, here's an
imagination that manages to incorporate a good deal of affection
for the old lady, the Muse, under its abrasively witty surface.

112

The Oxford Hysteria of English Poetry
ADRIAN MITCHELL

Back in the caveman days business was fair.
Used to turn up at Wookey Hole,
Plenty of action down the Hole
Nights when it wasn't raided.
They'd see my bear-gut harp
And the mess at the back of my eyes
And 'Right,' they'd say, 'make poetry.'
So I'd slam away at the three basic chords
And go into the act –
A story about sabre-toothed tigers with a comic hero;
A sexy one with an anti-wife-clubbing twist –
Good progressive stuff mainly,
Get ready for the Bronze Age, all that,
And soon it would be 'Bring out the woad!'
Yeah, woad. We used to get high on woad.

The Vikings only wanted sagas
Full of gigantic deadheads cutting off each other's vitals
Or Beowulf Versus the Bog People.
The Romans weren't much better,
Under all that armour you could tell they were soft
With their central heating
And poets with names like Horace.

Under the Normans the language began to clear,
Became a pleasure to write in,
Yes, write in, by now everyone was starting
To write down poems.
Well, it saved memorizing and improvising
And the peasants couldn't get hold of it.
Soon there were hundreds of us,
Most of us writing under the name of Geoffrey Chaucer.

Then suddenly we were knee-deep in sonnets.
Holinshed ran a headline:
BONANZA FOR BARDS.

It got fantastic –
Looning around from the bear-pit to the Globe,
All those freak-outs down the Mermaid,
Kit Marlowe coming on like Richard the Two,
A virgin Queen in a ginger wig
And English poetry in full whatsit –
Bloody fantastic, But I never found any time
To do any writing till Willy finally flipped –
Smoking too much of the special stuff
Sir Walter Raleigh was pushing.

Cromwell's time I spent on cultural committees.

Then Charles the Second swung down from the trees
And it was sexual medley time
And the only verses they wanted
Were epigrams on Chloe's breasts
But I only got published on the back of her left knee-cap.
Next came Pope and Dryden
So I went underground.
Don't mess with the mafia.

Then suddenly – WOOMF –
It was the Ro-man-tic Re-viv-al
And it didn't matter how you wrote,
All the public wanted was a hairy great image.
Before they'd even print you
You had to smoke opium, die of consumption,
Fall in love with your sister
Or drown in the Mediterranean (not at Brighton).
My publisher said: 'I'll have to remainder you
Unless you go and live in a lake or something
Like this bloke Wordsworth.'

After that there were about
A thousand years of Tennyson
Who got so bored with himself
That he changed his name
To Kipling at half-time.

Strange that Tennyson should be
Remembered for his poems really,
We always thought of him
As a golfer.

There hasn't been much time
For poetry since the 'twenties
What with leaving the Communist Church
To join the Catholic Party
And explaining why in the C.I.A. Monthly.
Finally I was given the Chair of Comparative Ambiguity
At Armpit University, Java.
It didn't keep me busy,
But it kept me quiet.
It seemed like poetry had been safely tucked up for the night.

Readers: John Shedden, Rose McBain

Full Selection:
Lochinvar, SIR WALTER SCOTT
Macbeth, WILLIAM SHAKESPEARE
November Eyes, JAMES ELROY FLECKER
Lines on the Death of Mr Levett, SAMUEL JOHNSON
Bagpipe Music, LOUIS MACNEICE
Thistles, TED HUGHES
A Study of Reading Habits, PHILIP LARKIN
Indoor Games Near Newbury, JOHN BETJEMAN
Do Not Go Gentle Into That Good Night, DYLAN THOMAS
Mort aux Chats, PETER PORTER
Dirge, KENNETH FEARING
The Oxford Hysteria of English Poetry, ADRIAN MITCHELL
The Flower, GEORGE HERBERT

BERNARD MILES

1971

What any presenter of 'With Great Pleasure' comes to realize, sooner or later, is that however urbane and well guarded his or her linking script may be, much of the essential personality is revealed by the choice of items. Sir Bernard came across as well balanced and 'all of a piece'. He claimed to be somewhat of a magpie in his reading, 'a bit here and a bit there' and confessed, as many have done, that making his selection took many hours, before delivering a script left over from a pile of his favourite passages 3 feet 6 inches high. He was clearly a warm and loving man, and his love of the sea and life on the water must have had no small a part to play in his drive to bring into being, on the banks of the Thames, the Mermaid Theatre.

One of the chief joys of this occasion is that I am doing it with my wife – indeed I am giving her the whole fee – and we are going to kick off with a pair of love letters, or at any rate letters about love.

The first was written on April 6th, 1761 by the famous Madame du Barry, Mistress of Louis XV, to a boyfriend in the days when she was still on the lower rungs of the ladder, serving in a millinery shop.

A Letter
MADAME DU BARRY

Yes, my dear friend, I have told you, and repeat it: I love you dearly. You certainly said the same thing to me, but on your side it is only impetuosity; directly after the first enjoyment, you

116

would think of me no more. I begin to know the world. I will tell you what I suggest, now: pay attention. I don't want to remain a shopgirl, but a little more my own mistress, and would therefore like to find someone to keep me. If I did not love you, I would try to get money from you; I would say to you, You shall begin by renting a room for me and furnishing it; only as you told me that you were not rich, you can take me to your own place. It will not cost you any more rent, nor more for your table and the rest of your housekeeping. To keep me and my head-dress will be the only expense, and for those give me three or four hundred francs a month, and that will include everything. Thus we could both live happily, and you would never again have to complain about my refusal. If you love me, accept this proposal; but if you do not love me, then let each of us try his luck elsewhere. Good-bye, I embrace you heartily.

Still on the never cloying subject of sex, I now turn to a delicious letter written by a wise and worldly man, the great American Benjamin Franklin, to a young anonymous friend who had written asking his advice on a very delicate personal problem. The date is June 25th, 1745.

A Letter
BENJAMIN FRANKLIN

My dear Friend,
I know of no medicine fit to diminish the violent natural inclination you mention, and if I did, I think I should not communicate it to you. Marriage is the proper remedy. It is the man and woman united that make the complete human being. A single man is an incomplete animal. He resembles the odd half of a pair of scissors.

But if you will not take this counsel and persist in thinking a commerce with sex inevitable, then I repeat my further advice that in all your amours you should prefer older women to younger ones.

My reasons are these:

1. Because when women cease to be handsome they study to be good. They learn to do a thousand services, small and great,

and are the most tender and useful of friends when you are sick.

2. Because through more experience they are more prudent and discreet. And if the affair should happen to be known, considerate people might be rather inclined to excuse an older woman, who would kindly take care of a younger man, and prevent his ruining his health and fortune among mercenary ladies of pleasure.

3. Because in every animal that walks upright the deficiency of the fluids that fill the muscles appears first in the highest parts, the lower parts continuing to the last as plump as ever. So that covering all above with a basket, and regarding only what is below the girdle, it is impossible of two women to tell an old one from a young one. In the dark all cats are grey.

4. Because the compunction is less. The having made a young girl miserable may give you frequent bitter reflection; none of which can attend the making an older woman happy.

5. And lastly, They are so grateful!

Now another letter, a serious one. It was written by the great Thomas Henry Huxley, contemporary and fellow worker with Charles Darwin, to the Reverend Charles Kingsley. Huxley had a favourite son who died young. This letter was written a few days after the boy's body had been put into the earth, in September 1860. Let me just add a confession of my own. Although I find it almost impossible to be a formal Christian, I am incorrigibly religious. And this letter expresses more perfectly than ever I could my own humble position in this eternal argument.

A Letter
THOMAS HENRY HUXLEY

As I stood beside the coffin of my little son the other day, with my mind bent on anything but disputation, the officiating minister read, as a part of his duty, the words, 'If the dead rise not again, let us eat and drink, for to-morrow we die.' I cannot tell you how inexpressibly they shocked me. St. Paul had neither wife nor child, or he must have known that his alternative involved a blasphemy against all that was best and noblest in human nature.

I could have laughed with scorn. What! Because I am face to face with irreparable loss, because I have given back to the source from whence it came, the cause of a great happiness, still retaining through all my life the blessings which have sprung and will spring from that cause, I am to renounce my manhood, and, howling, grovel in bestiality? Why, the very apes know better, and if you shoot their young, the poor brutes grieve their grief out and do not immediately seek distraction in a gorge.

Kicked into the world a boy without guide or training, or with worse than none, I confess to my shame that few men have drunk deeper of all kinds of sin than I. Happily, my course was arrested in time – before I had earned absolute destruction – and for long years I have been slowly and painfully climbing, with many a fall, towards better things. And when I look back, what do I find to have been the agents of my redemption? The hope of immortality or of future reward? I can honestly say that for these fourteen years such a consideration has not entered my head. No, I can tell you exactly what has been at work. Sartor Resartus led me to know that a deep sense of religion was compatible with the entire absence of theology. Secondly, science and her methods gave me a resting-place independent of authority and tradition. Thirdly, love opened up to me a view of the sanctity of human nature, and impressed me with a deep sense of responsibility.

If in the supreme moment when I looked down into my boy's grave my sorrow was full of submission and without bitterness, it is because these agencies have worked upon me, and not because I have ever cared whether my poor personality shall remain distinct for ever from the All from whence it came and whither it goes.

And thus, my dear Kingsley, you will understand what my position is. I may be quite wrong, and in that case I know I shall have to pay the penalty for being wrong. But I can only say with Martin Luther, 'Gott helfe mir, Ich kann nichts anders'. 'God help me, I can do no other'.

Many years ago Josephine and I went to Florence and into the Medici Chapel where lie Michelangelo's great marble figures of Night and Morning. We were the only two people there, it was in the evening, the attendant had gone off, and in the warm evening light the two great female figures really seemed alive, soft and warm, and I went up to one of them and gave way to the temptation to lay my hand between her thighs, hoping . . . certainly for the moment captured by the sense that this was not marble at all, but living flesh.

Well now, in the many choosings and re-choosings I made whilst putting together this programme, what I was never tempted to omit was three poems of Emily Dickinson. She was another extraordinary American, a New Englander, writing in the middle of the last century and endowed with a real genius for capturing the essence of an idea or situation in the most sharp and piercing language.

The Snake
EMILY DICKINSON

A narrow fellow on the grass
Occasionally rides;
You may have met him, – did you not,
His notice sudden is!
The grass divides as with a comb,
A spotted shaft is seen;
And then it closes at your feet
And opens further on.
He likes a boggy acre,
A floor too cool for corn.
Yet when a child, and barefoot,
I more than once, at noon,
Have passed, I thought, a whip-lash
Unbraiding in the sun
When stooping to secure it,
It wrinkled and was gone.
Several of nature's people
I know, and they know me;
I feel for them a transport
Of cordiality;
But never met this fellow,
Attended or alone,
Without a tighter breathing,
And zero at the bone.

120

The second poem communicates her delight in simply being alive:

Leaning Against the Sun
EMILY DICKINSON

I taste a liquor never brewed,
From tankards scooped in pearl;
Not all the vats upon the Rhine
Yield such an alcohol!
Inebriate of air am I,
And debauchee of dew,
Reeling, through endless summer days,
From inns of molten blue.
When landlords turn the drunken bee
Out of the foxglove's door,
When butterflies renounce their drams,
I shall but drink the more!
Till seraphs swing their snowy hats,
And saints to windows run,
To see the little tippler
Leaning against the sun!

The third poem describes the aftermath of death.

The Bustle in a House
EMILY DICKINSON

The bustle in a house,
    The morning after death
In solemnest of industries
    Enacted upon earth, –
The sweeping up the heart,
    And putting love away
We shall not want to use again
    Until eternity.

Now to a different kind of aftermath, an acute comment from a little known lady, Geraldine Jewsbury writing to Jane Carlyle in 1843. I'm sure you've been in love at one time or another and I'm

sure, like me, you've all fallen out of love, and this letter expresses the amazing reappraisal that one goes through when it's all
over and one's temperature is back to normal.

A Letter
GERALDINE JEWSBURY

When people are in love, they are in a magnetic state, and are
very much astonished at themselves when they come to their
senses. The other night the man who caused me more good and
evil feeling than I ever knew, before or since the three years his
influence lasted, ———, called here. I am frightened when I think
of the last year, and yet even that one is now like a tale I have read
– has no more to do with me, my present me, than the woes of
Dido! Well, as I said, that very man came in the other evening,
and stayed some time; he is really the most prosy, boring,
wearisome, commonplace person Nature has ever created. Once,
and not so long ago, that hour would have gilded a week, and
now it required an effort of politeness not to give an intelligible
hint to shorten his visit.

Now to a very favourite theme, the sea. Here is a letter from a boy
named Sam who served on the *Royal Sovereign* under Admiral
Collingwood. He's writing home to his father in a Yorkshire
village and he's just taken part in the battle of Trafalgar, one of the
most desperate and bloody of all sea actions.

A Letter
SAM

Honoured Father,
This comes to tell you I am alive and hearty except three fingers;
but that's not much, it might have been my head. I told brother
Tom I should like to see a greadly battle, and I have seen one, and
we have peppered the Combined Fleet rarely and they fought us
pretty tightish, for French and Spanish. Three of our mess are
killed, and four more of us winged. But to tell you the truth of it,
when the game began, I wished myself at Warnborough with my
plough again; but when they had given us one duster, and I
found myself snug and tight, I set to in good earnest, and thought

no more about being killed than if I were at Murrell Green Fair, and I was presently as busy and as black as a collier. How my fingers got knocked over-board I don't know but off they are, and I never missed them till I wanted them. You can see, by my writing, it was my left hand, so I can write to you and fight for my King and Country still. We have taken a rare parcel of ships, but the wind is so rough we cannot bring them home, else I should be rolling in money, so we are busy smashing 'em and blowing 'em up wholesale.

But our dear Admiral Nelson is killed. So we have paid pretty sharply for licking 'em. I never set eyes on him, for which I am both sorry and glad; for to be sure I should like to have seen him – but then all the men in our ship who have seen him are sicker than toads, they have done nothing but blast their eyes and cry ever since he was killed. God bless you! Chaps that fought like the devil, sit down and cry like a wench. I am still in Royal Sovereign, but Admiral [Collingwood] has left her, so she's like a horse without a bridle; he is in a frigate now so he can be here and there and everywhere, for he's as bold as a lion. For all he can cry! – I saw his tears with my own eyes, when the boat hailed us and said Lord Nelson was dead. So no more at present from your dutiful son.

Sam (Royal Sovereign) 1805

Readers: Sir Bernard and Lady Miles

Full Selection:
A Letter, MADAME DU BARRY
A Letter, BENJAMIN FRANKLIN
Ah, Are You Digging on My Grave, THOMAS HARDY
A Letter, THOMAS HENRY HUXLEY
Epitaph, CHURCHYARD AT BOLSOVER
The Elgin Marbles, BENJAMIN ROBERT HAYDON
The Snake, EMILY DICKINSON
Leaning Against the Sun, EMILY DICKINSON
The Bustle in a House, EMILY DICKINSON
A Letter, GERALDINE JEWSBURY
A Letter, SAILOR ON HMS 'ELGAR'

A Letter, SAM
Burning Shelley's Body, EDWARD TRELAWNEY
Life of Shelley, JEFFERSON HOGG
Portrait of the Artist as a Prematurely Old Man, OGDEN NASH
The Lowest Trees Have Tops . . . , SIR EDWARD DYER

DESMOND MORRIS

1979

Desmond Morris assured us in his programme that all the pieces he chose were from his library shelves. He acknowledged the temptation to rush out to the nearest bookshop and buy an armful of impressive classics 'to try and convince people how widely read you are', but resisted it. Most of the excerpts came from books he had bought a long time ago. Being a full-time writer, he conceded, gives him little time to read for pleasure. Nonetheless he retains a keen appreciation of poetry and the process of writing it.

It began for me when I was at boarding school and my botany master introduced me to the then modern poets. Auden and Isherwood became my firm favourites. I found their choice of images deeply impressive and they have lingered in my mind ever since.

The Dog Beneath the Skin
W. H. AUDEN and CHRISTOPHER ISHERWOOD

A man and a dog are entering a city: They are approaching a
    centre of culture:
First the suburban dormitories spreading over fields,

124

Villas on vegetation like saxifrage on stone,
Isolated from each other like cases of fever
And uniform in design, uniform as nurses.
To each a lean-to shed, containing a well-oiled engine of escape.
Section these dwellings: expose the life of a people
Living by law and the length of a reference,
See love in its disguises and the losses of the heart,
Cats and old silver inspire heroic virtues
And psychic fields, accidentally generated, destroy whole
    families.
Extraordinary tasks are set: a ploughman's hand acquires the
    most exquisite calligraphy,
A scheme is prepared for draining the North sea, with the aid of
    books from the local library:
One has a vision in the bathroom after a family quarrel: he
    kneels on the cork mat:
A naturalist leaves in a cab in time for the Breaking of the meres.
A youth with boils lies face down in bed, his mother over him;
Tenderly she squeezes from his trembling body the last dregs of
    his childhood.

Writer, be glib: please them with scenes of theatrical bliss and
    horror,
Whose own slight gestures tell their doom with a subtlety quite
    foreign to the stage.
For who patiently tell, tell of their sorrow
Without let or variation of season, streaming up in parallel from
    the little houses
And unabsorbed by their ironic treasures
Exerts on the rigid dome of the unpierced sky its enormous
    pressures?

I was beginning to find the natural world almost overwhelming –
there were so many species I wanted to study, and there just
wasn't enough time. I began to concentrate on reptiles and
amphibians – toads and snakes in particular. They were unpopu-
lar enough to appeal to my rebel spirit. I bought a small book of
animal poems and in it I was delighted to find a section dealing
with my favourite creatures, including this beautiful poem.

Snake
D. H. LAWRENCE

A snake came into my water-trough
On a hot, hot day, and I in pyjamas for the heat,
To drink there.

In the deep, strange-scented shade of the great dark carob tree
I came down the steps with my pitcher
And must wait, must stand and wait, for there he was at the
    trough before me.

He reached down from a fissure in the earth-wall in the gloom
And trailed his yellow-brown slackness soft-bellied down, over
    the edge of the stone trough
And rested his throat upon the stone bottom,
And where the water had dripped from the tap, in a small
    clearness,
He sipped with his straight mouth,
Softly drank through his straight gums, into his slack long body,
Silently.

Someone was before me at my water-trough,
And I, like a second comer, waiting.

He lifted his head from his drinking, as cattle do,
And looked at me vaguely, as drinking cattle do,
And flickered his two-forked tongue from his lips, and mused a
    moment,
And stooped and drank a little more,
Being earth-brown, earth-golden from the burning bowels of the
    earth.
On the day of Sicilian July, with Etna smoking.

The voice of my education said to me
He must be killed,
For in Sicily the black, black snakes are innocent, the gold are
    venomous.

And voices in me said, if you were a man
You would take a stick and break him now, and finish him off.

But must I confess how I liked him,
How glad I was he had come like a guest in quiet, to drink at my
   water-trough
And depart peaceful, pacified, and thankless,
Into the burning bowels of the earth?

Was it cowardice, that I dared not kill him?
Was it perversity, that I longed to talk to him?
Was it humility to feel so honoured?
I felt so honoured.

And yet those voices:
'If you were not afraid, you would kill him!'
And truly I was afraid, I was most afraid,
But even so, honoured still more
That he should seek my hospitality
From out the dark door of the secret earth.

He drank enough
And lifted his head, dreamily, as one who has drunken,
And flickered his tongue like a forked night on the air, so black,
Seeming to lick his lips,
And looked around like a god, unseeing, into the air,
And slowly turned his head,
And slowly, very slowly, as if thrice adream,
Proceeded to draw his slow length curving round
And climb again the broken bank of my wall-face.

And as he put his head into that dreadful hole,
And as he slowly drew up, snake-easing his shoulders, and
   entered farther,
A sort of horror, a sort of protest against his withdrawing into
   that horrid black hole,
Deliberately going into the blackness, and slowly drawing
   himself after,
Overcame me now his back was turned.

I looked around, I put down my pitcher,
I picked up a clumsy log
And threw it at the water-trough with a clatter.
I think it did not hit him,

127

But suddenly that part of him that was left behind convulsed in
    undignified haste,
Writhed like lightning, and was gone
Into the black hole, the earth-lopped fissure in the wall-front,
At which, in the intense still noon, I stared with fascination.

And immediately I regretted it.
I thought how paltry, how vulgar, what a mean act!
I despised myself and the voices of my accursed human
    education.

And I thought of the albatross,
And I wished he would come back, my snake.
For he seemed to me again like a king,
Like a king in exile, uncrowned in the underworld,
Now due to be crowned again.

And so, I missed my chance with one of the lords
Of life.
And I have something to expiate:
A pettiness.

I was quite oblivious of any Freudian undertones there might
have been in that poem. To me it was simply a perfect comment
on the clash between the joy of observing nature and the desire to
interfere with it. It was a conflict that was very much present in
my own life and it was only slowly, very slowly, that the urge to
watch overpowered the juvenile excitement of hunting, catching
and keeping animals. I spent more and more time just sitting,
looking at animals in the wild and, as the years went by, there
were times when I felt I even preferred their company to that of
my own species. Walt Whitman seemed to echo these feelings in
this famous, short poem.

Animals
WALT WHITMAN

I think I could turn and live with animals,
    they are so placid and self-contain'd,
I stand and look at them long and long.
They do not sweat and whine about their condition.

They do not lie awake in the dark and weep for their sins,
They do not make me sick discussing their duty to God.
Not one is dissatisfied, not one is demented
    with the mania of owning things,
Not one kneels to another nor to his kind
    that lived thousands of years ago.
Not one is respectable or unhappy over the whole earth.

Although I liked the idea behind that poem, I was a bit worried about how he could be so sure that animals were never unhappy, or dissatisfied. And I had seen racehorses steaming after a race, so that I knew that some of them could sweat. He seemed to have got some of his facts wrong, but his heart was in the right place, so I forgave him. But my own studies, when I eventually became a zoology student at university, were more and more concerned with the objective analysis of animal behaviour and less and less with animal poetry. Later at Oxford I came under the influence of the great ethologists Niko Tinbergen and Konrad Lorenz. Lorenz, I remember, told me that the only time animals made him laugh was when they were making *people* look ridiculous.

Every meeting with Konrad was full of laughter – in fact I think it's true that almost every great man I have encountered, no matter how serious in his public role, has always been full of humour in his private moments. I have found this true of scientists and artists alike. When I was lucky enough to meet Dylan Thomas, shortly before his last fatal trip to America, he was no exception. And for that reason, in choosing something from his writings, I have selected the one occasion on which he allowed himself to be outrageously funny in print. Tony Hubbard, a friend of mine from my army days, had started a small magazine called *Circus*. It didn't last long, but in its first two issues, in April and May 1950, he persuaded Dylan to contribute a double piece on 'How to be a Poet'. Dylan called it *The Ascent of Parnassus Made Easy, a Worldly Lecture in Two Parts*. Here are brief extracts from each part, in which he lampoons two imaginary poets.

The Ascent of Parnassus Made Easy
DYLAN THOMAS

I do not intend to ask, let alone to answer, the question, 'Is poetry a Good Thing?' but only, 'Can Poetry Be Made Good Business?'

I shall, to begin with, introduce to you, with such comments as may or may not be necessary, a few of the main types of poets who have made the social and financial grade.

First, though not in order of importance, is the poet who has emerged docketed 'lyrical', from the Civil Service. He can be divided, so far as his physical appearance goes, into two types. He is either thin, not to say of a shagged out appearance, with lips as fulsome, sensual, and inviting as a hen's ovipositor, bald from all too maculate birth, his eyes made small and reddened by reading books in French, a language he cannot understand, in an attic in the provinces while young and repellent, his voice like the noise of a mouse's nail on tinfoil, his nostrils transparent, his breath grey; or else he is jowled and bushy, with curved pipe and his nose full of dottle, the look of all Sussex in his stingo'd eyes, his burry tweeds smelling of the dogs he loathes, with a voice like a literate airedale's that has learnt its vowels by correspondence course, and an intimate friend of Chesterton's whom he never met. Dropped into the Civil Service at an age when many of our young poets now are running away to Broadcasting House, today's equivalent of the Sea, he is at first lost to sight in the mountains of red tape which, in future years, he is so mordantly, though with a wry and puckered smile, to dismiss in a paragraph in his *Around and About My Shelves*. After a few years, he begins to peer out from the forms and files in which he leads his ordered nibbling life, and picks up a cheese crumb here, a dropping there, in his ink-stained thumbs. And soon he learns that a poem in a Civil Service magazine is, if not a step up the ladder, at least a lick in the right direction. And he writes a poem. It is, of course, about Nature: it confesses a wish to escape from the humdrum routine and embrace the unsophisticated life of the farm labourer: he desires, though without scandal, to wake up with the birds: he expresses the opinion that a ploughshare, not a pen, best fits his little strength: a decorous pantheist, he is one with the rill, the rhyming mill, the rosy-bottomed milkmaid, the russet-cheeked rat-catcher, swains, swine, pipits, pippins. You can smell the country in his poem, the fields, the flowers, the armpits of Triptolemus, the barns, the byres, the hay and, most of all, the corn.

And now we must move to see for a moment a very different kind of poet, whom we shall call Cedric. To follow in Cedric's footsteps – (he'd love you to, and would never call a policeman unless it was that frightfully sinister sergeant you see sometimes in Mecklenburgh Square, just like an El Greco) – you must be born twilightly into the middle classes, go to one of the correct schools – (which, of course, you must loathe, for it is essential, from the first, to be misunderstood) – and arrive at the University with your reputation already established as a coming poet and looking, if possible, something between a Guards' officer and a fashionable photographer's doxy.

So here is Cedric, known already to the discerning few for his sensitive poems about golden limbs, sun-jewelled fronds, the ambrosia of the first shy kiss in the delicate-traceried caverns of the moon (really the school boot-cupboard), at the threshold of fame and the world laid out before him like a row of balletomanes. If this were the 'twenties', Cedric's first book of poems, published while he was still an undergraduate, might be called *Asps and Lutes*. It would be nostalgic for a life that never was. It would be world-weary. (He once saw the world, out of a train carriage window: it looked unreal.) It would be a carefully garish mixture, a cunningly evocative pudding full of plums pulled from the Sitwells and Sacheverell other people, a mildly cacophonous hothouse of exotic horticultural and comic-erotic bric-a-brac, from which I extract these typical lines:

> 'A cornucopia of phalluses
> Cascade on the vermillion palaces
> In arabesques and syrup
>   rigadoons;
> Quince-breasted Circes of the
>   zenanas
> Do catch this rain of cherry-
>   wigged bananas
> And saraband beneath the raspberry
>   moons.'

Readers: Freddie Jones, Brenda Kaye

Full Selection:
The Dog Beneath the Skin, W. H. AUDEN and CHRISTOPHER ISHERWOOD
The Beast in Me, JAMES THURBER
Snake, D. H. LAWRENCE
Animals, WALT WHITMAN
The Ascent of Parnassus Made Easy, DYLAN THOMAS
Children's Letters to God
Discretion, ROGER McGOUGH
Men, DOROTHY PARKER
Guarantee, PHILIP OAKES
In His Own Write, JOHN LENNON
The Fate of Felicity Fark in the Land of the Media, CLIVE JAMES
A World on the Wane, CLAUDE LÉVI-STRAUSS

PETER NICHOLS

1983

On the opening night of one of Peter Nichols' plays I found myself on the outside balcony of a theatre in Shaftesbury Avenue placing smiley lanterns on the balustrade. The evening had started uneventfully enough. I had been sent by 'Kaleidoscope' to interview the playwright, record a brief scene with Albert Finney and the other actors and watch the play. Nichols was charming, if nervous, whilst the cast were in high good humour. The producer was Michael Medwin and the idea of the lanterns was his. Thirty minutes before curtain-up he realized that there was no-one left to undertake this precarious task but him and me. Thus for the first time in the West End I had my face if not my name in lights!

Ours was not a literary family and my staple reading as a boy was a set of Odhams Press editions of children's classics, which luckily included *Tales of Robin Hood, Stories from Grimm*, Hans Andersen and the *Arabian Nights, Gulliver's Travels* and *Robinson Crusoe*. Otherwise I remember only the *William* books by Richmal Crompton, an American publication called *Believe It Or Not* and Rudyard Kipling's *Just-So Stories*. I still have my copy of the last, a present from an uncle for my eighth birthday. I wish I'd kept *Believe It Or Not*, which was a sort of freak show in book form, a precursor of *The Guinness Book of Records*, but with more emphasis on savage tribes who played football with a skull or how many people could stand on each other's heads inside the Statue of Liberty.

So, nothing from my childhood but a poem *about* children. It's on the birth of Christ and it's by the sixteenth-century Jesuit, Robert Southwell, who was executed for his allegiance to the Pope in 1595. His devotional poems are eloquent assertions of faith over common sense. I wish I could believe that innocence and goodness will prevail, but all my observation of life tells me they won't. Southwell says they will in his poem.

This Little Babe
ROBERT SOUTHWELL

This little babe so few days old
Is come to rifle Satan's fold;
All earth doth at his presence quake
Though he himself for cold do shake;
For in this weak, unarmèd wise
The Gates of Hell he will surprise.

With tears he fights and wins the field,
His naked breast stands for a shield;
His battering shot are babeish cries,
His arrows looks weeping eyes,
His martial ensigns Cold and Need
And feeble flesh his warrior's steed.

His camp is pitchèd in a stall,
His bulwark but a broken wall;
The crib his trench, haystacks his stakes,

Of shepherds he his muster makes;
And thus, as sure his bow to wound,
The angels' trumps alarum sound.

My soul, with Christ join thou in fight;
Stick to the tents that he hath pight.
Within his crib is surest ward;
This little Babe will be thy guard.
If thou wilt foil thy foes with joy,
Then flit not from this heavenly Boy.

Does the poet's subsequent torture and death prove he was
wrong? Does human history ever since? Well, I'm an atheist but
can still be moved to tears by Handel's *Messiah*. My religious
experience as a child can be quickly dealt with. For two weeks I
was a chorister in our parish church of St Bartholomew. One day
during morning service the organist suffered such noisy wind
that I literally fainted with laughter. I woke up being carried from
the church head down by the muscular vicar. After that I seldom
entered a church again until I started looking at architecture in my
aesthetic twenties.

Falling in love was another experience I somehow missed. Everyone around me in wartime England was pursuing somebody else
as though sex had just been discovered. Which, in many cases, it
probably had. The quondam – I like that word, it means previously – the quondam sober women of Ashley Down were hurling
themselves at successive waves of American soldiers now billeted
in the orphanage. And I hung out in the milk bars feeding the
juke-boxes and hoping some of that blatant sexiness would rub
off on me. It's hard to realize how prim the official culture was.
Real life was bursting out all over, GIs of all shades from sallow to
black were buying British womanhood with Lucky Strikes and
nylons, but not a hint of it got on to the BBC and not much more
into the papers. This is perhaps why people of my age are
generally fond of erotic literature, soft porn and what was known
in my family as 'language'. If I so much as said 'damn' my father
told me not to use language. How else were we to communicate?

Barking? Humming? Whistling? It came as such a relief when, during the sixties, we could at last unbutton our lips and talk dirty. I was amazed to find there was a wealth of filth going back to the dawn of civilization. The British Museum's full of it. The Vatican has one of the best collections. But most of it – from Ovid to 'Eskimo Nell' we still can't read on the air.

Here's one, though, a mild and ingenious poem by e. e. cummings. It's about as rude as I can get on this so-called programme of pleasure.

may i feel said he
e. e. cummings

may i feel said he
(i'll squeal said she
just once said he)
it's fun said she

(may i touch said he
how much said she
a lot said he)
why not said she

(let's go said he
not too far said she
what's too far said he
where you are said she)

may i stay said he
(which way said she
like this said he
if you kiss said she

may i move said he
is it love said she)
if you're willing said he
(but you're killing said she

but it's life said he
but your wife said she
now said he)
ow said she

(tiptop said he
don't stop said she
oh no said he)
go slow said she

(cccome? said he
ummm said she)
you're divine! said he
(you are Mine said she)

My wife and I were both teachers when we married, but my wife's dowry was a pressure cooker and her superannuation, which we soon cashed to eke out my income as a professional playwright. I've been lucky enough to earn a living most of the time. We've not always been well off but never desperately poor either. In days gone by, of course, writers usually were – poets particularly. Samuel Johnson wrote of the seventeenth-century Samuel Butler: 'A man whose name can only perish with his language. The mode and place of his education are unknown, the events of his life are variously related and all that can be told with certainty is, that he was poor.' Some years after his death, a monument was raised to him in Westminster Abbey and here's an epigram by Samuel Wesley to celebrate that event.

Epigram SAMUEL WESLEY

While Butler, needy wretch, was yet alive
No generous patron would a dinner give.
See him when starved to death and turned to dust
Presented with a monumental bust.
The poet's fate is here in emblem shown,
He asked for bread and he received a stone.

Mind you, he'd not have earned that much more bread reciting verse on Radio 4 instead.

We began with birth and we end with death. Which is all any of us can be sure of. Even Falstaff. A prose passage which shows the superstar scripter Shakespeare not only describing the dying man but, by the tone of voice, the character and attitude of Mistress Quickly, who speaks it. One of their friends wishes he were with the dead knight whether he's in Heaven or in Hell.

136

King Henry V
WILLIAM SHAKESPEARE

Nay, sure, he's not in hell: he's in Arthur's bosom, if ever man went to Arthur's bosom. A' made a finer end, and went away, an it had been any Christom child; a' parted even just between twelve and one, even at the turning o' the tide: for after I saw him fumble with the sheets, and play with flowers and smile upon his fingers' ends, I knew there was but one way; for his nose was as sharp as a pen, and a' babbled of green fields. *How now, Sir John?* quoth I: *what, man! be o' good cheer.* So a' cried out – *God, God, God!* three or four times. Now I, to comfort him, bid him a' should not think of God; I hoped there was no need to trouble himself with any such thoughts yet. So a' bade me lay more clothes on his feet: I put my hand into the bed and felt them, and they were as cold as any stone; then I felt to his knees, and so upward, and upward, and all was as cold as any stone.

I hope this selection has helped you understand, if not share, the sentiments of Logan Pearsall Smith whose last words were:

'People say that life is the thing but I prefer reading.'

Readers: Eileen Atkins, Joe Melia

Full Selection:
This Little Babe, ROBERT SOUTHWELL
Sarah Byng, HILAIRE BELLOC
Great Expectations, CHARLES DICKENS
Critical Essays, GEORGE ORWELL
In Praise of the Good Old Flag, BILLY BENNETT
Weekend in the Country, IRA GERSHWIN
Symptom Recital, DOROTHY PARKER
may i feel said he, e. e. cummings
Epigram, SAMUEL WESLEY
For Sidney Bechet, PHILIP LARKIN
Poppy (John Companee), PETER NICHOLS
Election Fever, ROGER WODDIS

The Surgeon at 2 A.M., SYLVIA PLATH
The Little Things You Do Together, STEPHEN SONDHEIM
King Henry V, WILLIAM SHAKESPEARE
Famous Sayings, WOODY ALLEN, WILLIAM PITT, DOROTHY
PARKER, LORD PALMERSTON, LOGAN PEARSALL SMITH

MARY O'HARA

1986

Mary O'Hara's story is well known through her autobiography and innumerable interviews: leaving the convent to which she had retreated for many years after the death of her first husband, she returned to the world in order to resume a successful career as a singer. Her first broadcast at that time was produced by Madeau Stewart for Radio 3. As the studio manager I enjoyed the challenge of recording voice and harp in a way that gave proper clarity to both elements, and I enjoyed meeting this warm woman who had obviously suffered much, come to terms with it and was confident that she was now doing the right thing. I did not meet her again until the recording of 'With Great Pleasure' in March 1986. What I remember most is the laughter. Her good humour and pleasure in life were captivating. A minute before we were due on stage we were both convulsed over some line or other in the script. Later, over dinner, she, her new husband and Kate Binchy told Irish jokes as only the Irish can. It was a fine evening.

Some people fall in love with *The Wind in the Willows* when they are small children. I was in my early twenties when I was first bowled over by it and it has remained a huge favourite with me ever since. The little otter has gone missing, and Rat and Mole set

138

out in their boat determined to find him. And in so doing they have the following mysterious experience.

The Wind in the Willows
KENNETH GRAHAME

Breathless and transfixed the Mole stopped rowing as the liquid run of that glad piping broke on him like a wave, caught him up, and possessed him utterly. He saw the tears on his comrade's cheeks, and bowed his head and understood. For a space they hung there, brushed by the purple loosestrife that fringed the bank; then the clear imperious summons that marched hand-in-hand with the intoxicating melody imposed its will on Mole, and mechanically he bent to his oars again. And the light grew steadily stronger, but no bands sang as they were wont to do at the approach of dawn; and but for the heavenly music all was marvellously still.

On either side of them, as they glided onwards, the rich meadow-grass seemed that morning of a freshness and a greenness unsurpassable. Never had they noticed the roses so vivid, the willow-herb so riotous, the meadow-sweet so odorous and pervading. Then the murmur of the approaching weir began to hold the air, and they felt a consciousness that they were nearing the end, whatever it might be, that surely awaited their expedition.

A wide half-circle of foam and glinting lights and shining shoulders of green water, the great weir closed the backwater from bank to bank, troubled all the quiet surface with twirling eddies and floating foam-streaks, and deadened all other sounds with its solemn and soothing rumble. In midmost of the stream, embraced in the weir's shimmering armspread, a small island lay anchored, fringed close with willow and silver birch and alder. Reserved, shy, but full of significance, it hid whatever it might hold behind a veil, keeping it till the hour should come, and, with the hour, those who were called and chosen.

Slowly, but with no doubt or hesitation whatever, and in something of a solemn expectancy, the two animals passed through the broken, tumultuous water and moored their boat at the flowery margin of the island. In silence they landed and pushed through the blossom and scented herbage and undergrowth that led up to the level ground, till they stood on a little lawn of a marvellous green, set round with Nature's own orchard-trees – crab apple, wild cherry, and sloe.

'This is the place of my song-dream, the place the music played to me,' whispered the Rat, as if in a trance. 'Here, in this holy place, here if anywhere, surely we shall find Him!'

Then suddenly the Mole felt a great Awe fall upon him, an awe that turned his muscles to water, bowed his head, and rooted his feet to the ground. It was no panic terror – indeed he felt wonderfully at peace and happy – but it was an awe that smote and held him and, without seeing, he knew that it could only mean that some august Presence was very, very near. With difficulty he turned to look for his friend, and saw him at his side cowed, stricken, and trembling violently. And still there was utter silence in the populous bird-haunted branches around them; and still the light grew and grew.

Perhaps he would never have dared to raise his eyes, but that, though the piping was now hushed, the call and the summons seemed still dominant and imperious. He might not refuse, were Death himself waiting to strike him instantly, once he had looked with mortal eye on things rightly kept hidden. Trembling he obeyed, and raised his humble head; and then, in that utter clearness of the imminent dawn, while Nature, flushed with fullness of incredible colour, seemed to hold her breath for the event, he looked into the very eyes of his Friend and Helper; saw the backward sweep of the curved horns, gleaming in the growing daylight; saw the stern, hooked nose between the kindly eyes that were looking down on them humorously, while the bearded mouth broke into a half-smile at the corners; saw the rippling muscles on the arm that lay across the broad chest, the long supple hand still holding the pan-pipes only just fallen away from the parted lips; saw the splendid curves of the shaggy limbs disposed in majestic ease on the sward; saw, last of all, nestling between his very hooves, sleeping soundly in entire peace and contentment, the little, round, podgy, childish form of the baby otter. All this he saw, for one moment breathless and intense, vivid on the morning sky; and still, as he looked, he lived; and still, as he lived, he wondered.

'Rat!' he found breath to whisper, shaking. 'Are you afraid?'

'Afraid?' murmured the Rat, his eyes shining with unutterable love. 'Afraid! Of *Him*? O, never, never! And yet – and yet – O, Mole, I am afraid!'

Then the two animals, crouching to the earth, bowed their heads and did worship.

Sudden and magnificent, the sun's broad golden disc showed itself over the horizon facing them; and the first rays, shooting across the level water-meadows, took the animals full in the eyes and dazzled them. When they were able to look once more, the Vision had vanished, and the air was full of the carol of birds that hailed the dawn.

The ability to laugh, especially at oneself, and not take oneself, one's work, one's life too seriously is a recipe for sanity. George Bernard Shaw with typical Shavian wit wrote that seriousness is a small man's affectation of greatness. I think I know what he meant. Sometimes if I find myself getting depressed about something and need to see things in perspective I go back to a book by Hugo Rahner called *Man at Play*. It's quite a powerful antidote.

Man at Play
HUGO RAHNER

The 'grave-merry' man is really always two men in one: he is a man with an easy gaiety of spirit, one might almost say a man of spiritual elegance, a man who feels himself to be living in invincible security; but he is also a man of tragedy, a man of ridiculous masks of the game of life and has taken the measure of the cramping boundaries of our earthly existence.

And so, only one who can fuse these two contradictory elements into a spiritual unity is indeed a man who truly plays. If he is only the first of these two things, we must write him down as a frivolous person who has, precisely, played himself out. If he is only the second, then we must account him as one who cannot conquer despair. It is the synthesis of the two things that makes Homo Ludens, the 'grave-merry' man, the man with a gentle sense of humour who laughs despite his tears, and finds in all earthly mirth a sediment of insufficience. . . .

The man who truly plays is, therefore, first of all, a man in whom seriousness and gaiety are mingled; and, indeed, at the bottom of all play there lies a tremendous secret. All play – just as much as every task which we set ourselves to master with real earnestness of purpose – is an attempt to approximate to the Creator, who performs his work with the divine seriousness which its meaning and purpose demand, and yet with the spontaneity and effortless skill of the great artist he is, creating because he wills to create and not because he must. . . .

This happy mingling of the light-hearted and the serious is a flower that grows only midway betwixt heaven and earth – in the man who loves this bright and colourful world and yet can smile at it, who knows in his heart that it has proceeded from God but also knows its limits. Within those limits, and because of them, things knock into each other, thus producing comedy – but also tragedy. These may annoy us; we can react angrily or we can accept them with calm good humour. They can disconcert us and still, at the same time, delight us in our vision directed always towards the Logos in his 'co-fashioning' action, for it is in him that everything has its source and it is towards the vision of him that all our play ultimately tends.

Nowadays we are all very conscious of the necessity to preserve the balance of nature that's so threatened by so-called progress. Perhaps we could be forgiven for thinking that such laudable concern was invented by Greenpeace – certainly any stories that I read as a child wouldn't have prepared me for regarding the American Indian as a forerunner for Greenpeace.

Letter to the President of the United States in 1885
CHIEF SEATHL

The Great Chief in Washington sends word that he wishes to buy our land. The Great Chief also sends us words of friendship and good will. This is kind of him, since we know he has little need for our friendship in return. But we will consider your offer, for we know that if we do not do so, the white man may come with guns and take our land. What Chief Seathl says, the Great Chief in Washington can count on as truly as our white brothers can count on the return of the seasons. My words are like the stars – they do not set.

How can you buy or sell the sky – the warmth of the land? The idea is strange to us. Yet we do not own the freshness of the air or the sparkle of the water. How can you buy them from us? We will decide in our time. Every part of this earth is sacred to my people. Every shining pine needle, every sandy shore, every mist in the dark woods, every clearing and humming insect is holy in the memory and experience of my people.

We know that the white man does not understand our ways. One portion of the land is the same to him as the next, for he is a stranger who comes in the night and takes from the land whatever he needs. The earth is not his brother, but his enemy, and when he has conquered it, he moves on. He leaves his fathers' graves behind and he does not care. He kidnaps the earth from his children. He does not care. His fathers' graves and his children's birthright are forgotten. His appetite will devour the earth and leave behind only a desert. The sight of your cities pains the eyes of the redman. But perhaps it is because the redman is a savage and does not understand. . . .

There is no quiet place in the white man's cities. No place to hear the leaves of spring or the rustle of insects' wings. But because perhaps I am a savage and do not understand the clatter only seems to insult the ears. And what is there to life if a man cannot hear the lovely cry of the whippoorwill or the argument of the frogs around a pond at night? The Indian prefers the soft sound of the wind darting over the face of the pond, and the smell of the wind itself cleansed by a mid-day rain, or scented with pinion pine. The air is precious to the redman. For all things share the same breath – the beasts, the trees, the man. The white man does not seem to notice the air he breathes. Like a man dying for many days, he is numb to the smell of his own stench. . . .

When the last redman has vanished from the earth, and the memory is only the shadow of a cloud moving across the prairie, these shores and forests will still hold the spirits of my people, for they love the earth as the newborn loves its mother's heartbeat.

If we sell you our land, love it as we've loved it. Care for it as we've cared for it. Hold in your mind the memory of the land, as it is when you take it. And with all your strength, with all your might, and with all your heart preserve it for your children, and love it as God loves us all. One thing we know – our God is the same God. This earth is precious to him. Even the white man cannot be exempt from the common destiny.

Readers: Sion Probert, Kate Binchy

Full Selection:
The Wind in the Willows, KENNETH GRAHAME
The Rat, GEORGE SCOTT MONCRIEFF
Mother and Son, LIAM O'FLAHERTY
Reflection, R. J. SELIG
Man at Play, HUGO RAHNER
The Lost World of the Kalahari, LAURENS VAN DER POST
If I Should Go Before the Rest of You, JOYCE GRENFELL
And Were You Pleased, LORD DUNSANY
Under Milk Wood, DYLAN THOMAS
Letter to the President of the United States in 1885, CHIEF SEATHL
The Best of Myles, FLANN O'BRIEN
The Fellowship of the Ring, J. R. R. TOLKIEN
In God's Underground, RICHARD WURMBRAND
The Little Prince, ANTOINE DE SAINTE-EXUPERY
Gitanjali, RABINDRANATH TAGORE

PETER PEARS

1986

As a young photographic printer working in Television Centre in 1962 I remember rushing home from work to be in time to listen to the first performance of Benjamin Britten's War Requiem. *As Peter Pears sang the opening line from Wilfred Owen, 'What passing-bells for those who die as cattle', it was as if the air were filled with a sense of reconciliation and of hope for the future. The war was finally over. That strange excitement remains with me to this day and twenty-four years after that evening it was a great thrill for me to have the opportunity of meeting Sir Peter. He was, of course, with Britten a familiar figure in Aldeburgh and the affection in which he was held by the audience as he sat on the stage, in his favourite armchair specially brought in for the occasion, was unmistakable. When he spoke it was as if his voice could scarcely refrain from song. It was his last broadcast.*

I have been a singer for fifty years and in the course of those years I have got to love certain music and not love other music quite so much. I started singing these pieces fifty years ago and I sang them across America and I've got very fond of them. They are from the best period of English music, the Elizabethan time. I think they're beautiful.

Four Madrigals of Six Parts
THOMAS WEELKES

Thule, the period of cosmography,
Doth vaunt of Hecla, whose sulphurious fire
Doth melt the frozen clime and thaw the sky;
Trinacrian Aetna's flames ascend not higher.
These things seem wondrous, yet more wondrous I,
Whose heart with fear doth freeze, with love doth fry.

The Andalusian merchant, that returns
Laden with cochineal and China dishes,
Reports in Spain how strangely Fogo burns
Amidst an ocean full of flying fishes.
These things seem wondrous, yet more wondrous I
Whose heart with fear doth freeze, with love doth fry.

The First Set of Madrigals
ORLANDO GIBBONS

The silver swan, who living had no note,
When death approached unlocked her silent throat;
Leaning her breast against the reedy shore,

145

Thus sung her first and last, and sung no more:
Farewell, all joys: O death, come close mine eyes;
More geese than swans now live, more fools than wise.

What is our life? a play of passion
Our mirth the music of division.
Our mothers' wombs the tiring-houses be,
Where we are dressed for this short comedy.
Heaven the judicious sharp spectator is,
That sits and marks still who doth act amiss.
Our graves that hide us from the searching sun
Are like drawn curtains when the play is done.
Thus march we, playing, to our latest rest,
Only we die in earnest, that's no jest.

The Second Set of Madrigals
JOHN WILBYE

Draw on, sweet Night, best friend unto those cares
That do arise from painful melancholy.
My life so ill through want of comfort fares,
That unto thee I consecrate it wholly.
Sweet night, draw on! My griefs when they be told
To shades and darkness, find some ease from paining.
And while thou all in silence dost enfold,
I then shall have best time for my complaining.

One of the great loves of my youth was Jane Austen and I had the idea that we might have had a whole first chapter of one of her great books because in her first chapter she always seems to put the stage absolutely right for the rest of the book: you are told what so-and-so is, how another is a terrible snob and so on, but that's rather long so we didn't choose that. I decided on more juvenile Jane Austen, from an old album not often seen.

The Adventures of Mr Harley
JANE AUSTEN

A short but interesting Tale, is with all imaginable Respect inscribed to Mr Francis William Austen Midshipman on board his Majestys Ship the Perseverance by his Obedient Servant, THE AUTHOR

146

Mr Harley was one of many Children. Destined by his father for the Church & by his Mother for the Sea, desirous of pleasing both, he prevailed on Sir John to obtain for him a Chaplaincy on board a Man of War. He accordingly cut his Hair and sailed.

In half a year he returned & set off in the Stage Coach for Hogsworth Green, the seat of Emma. His fellow travellers were, A man without a Hat, Another with two, An old maid & a young Wife.

This last appeared about 17 with fine dark Eyes & an elegant Shape; in short Mr Harley soon found out, that she was his Emma & recollected he had married her a few weeks before he left England.

FINIS

One of the oddities about Jane Austen was that she was rather an admirer of our local poet, George Crabbe. It is difficult to see them getting on really because she obviously had a tremendous sense of humour, 'though kept under, but he I don't think had a sense of humour at all. One thing we do know about him is that he did not like Aldeburgh although he was born here and as one way, I think, of getting his own back on Aldeburgh he wrote this poem.

Marsh Flowers
GEORGE CRABBE

Here the strong mallow strikes her slimy root, .
Here the dull nightshade hangs her deadly fruit;
On hills of dust the henbane's faded green,
And pencill'd flower of sickly scent is seen.
Here on its wiry stem, in rigid bloom
Grows the salt lavender that lacks perfume.

At the wall's base the fiery nettle springs
With fruit globose and fierce with poison'd stings;
In ev'ry chink delights the fern to grow,
With glossy leaf and tawny bloom below;
The few dull flowers that o'er the place are spread
Partake the nature of their fenny bed,
These with our seaweeds rolling up and down
Form the contracted Flora of our town.

Readers: Peter Pears, Julia Lang

Full Selection:
Four Madrigals of Six Parts, THOMAS WEELKES
The First Set of Madrigals, ORLANDO GIBBONS
The Second Set of Madrigals, JOHN WILBYE
The Moth and the Star, JAMES THURBER
The Glass in the Field, JAMES THURBER
The Adventures of Mr Harley, JANE AUSTEN
Marsh Flowers, GEORGE CRABBE
Dunwich: Winter Visit Along, JOHN MATHIAS
Two Ladies, JOHN MATHIAS
An Angel in Blythburgh Church, PETER PORTER
O Lurcher-Loving Collier, W. H. AUDEN
XXVII, W. H. AUDEN
Graveyard in Norfolk, SYLVIA TOWNSEND WARNER
Gloriana Dying, SYLVIA TOWNSEND WARNER
December 31st St Silvester, SYLVIA TOWNSEND WARNER

LAURENS VAN DER POST

1978

Unlike 'Desert Island Discs', 'With Great Pleasure' never invites a
presenter back for a second go. That at any rate is the theory. In fact two
people have found themselves twice talking to Radio 4 listeners about
their favourite poetry and prose: John Mortimer reappeared in another

*guise for an 'April Fool' edition, whilst Laurens van der Post had taken
part some years previously for another producer. The second invitation
was an accident, but was accepted nonetheless. For the more recent
programme this farmer, soldier, explorer, writer and adviser to the heir to
the throne acknowledged his 'enormous unrepayable debt to the written
literature of the world' but decided to lay his emphasis on to the 'literature
out of which all literature arose, the spoken, the unwritten literature of
the world'.*

I was fortunate to be born into an Africa where one had an
immense amount of this sort of literature around. It was always
around us. I was fortunate also that I was in contact daily with
people who thought that story-telling was not just for children,
that it was just as much for the old, that somehow this was one of
the most important mechanisms in life. Years later when I was
exploring the Kalahari Desert I found the people there would tell
me everything except their stories. They knew instinctively that
the story was their most precious possession and that the most
dangerous thing you could do was to let a stranger in on to their
stories, because if a stranger got in on to the story he might mock
it, he might take it away, and I realized that we have killed off
scores of civilizations and peoples merely by taking away their
story. It's a peril which confronts the world today, everywhere
people's stories are being taken away from them and as a result
they are losing a sense of meaning and losing their sense of
direction. As a result of all this inherited sense of the importance
of the story my childhood memories are crowded with stories,
but there was one story to which I'd turn again and again because
it seemed to me that all literature, even the most sophisticated
and highly orchestrated kind, is concerned with the theme of this
story; it's a story told to me by my old bushman nurse so far back
that I can't even remember my exact age. It's *The Story of the Great
White Bird* and she had a special tone in her voice when she told
this story.

The Story of the Great White Bird
TRADITIONAL

There was a hunter once and, because he was young and beautiful and utterly hunter, he was loved by everyone. He was the

greatest provider of food for his people. Because, feeling himself to be utterly hunter and utterly loved, his arrows and his spears never failed to find their mark. Then one day he felt himself called in a dream to go hunting in the forest of Duk-A-Duk-Duk. This forest was called Duk-A-Duk-Duk because it was so thick and so dark that people, once in a forest feeling itself to be utterly dark, found their hearts going duk-a-duk on account of it.

So they watched him go early in the morning, not without fear. But knowing him to be so utterly hunter they told themselves that their fears were foolish. The sun, feeling itself to be hot, was fierce and strong, and towards noon the hunter, feeling himself to be thirsty, branched from the track of an animal he was stalking and followed the voices of the purple doves he knew would lead him to water. Soon he came to a clearing where there was a deep pool of water. The water was still and so full of the blue of the day that it was as if he was looking into another sky at his feet. He knelt down to drink, but just before his lips touched the water suddenly, dazzling and swift, on the surface there appeared the reflection of a great white shining bird. He looked up quickly but the sky was empty and for a moment he wondered whether he had not dreamt it all because of the strangeness, the size, the whiteness and speed of the bird. But once back in the forest, he found he could not go on hunting. He no longer saw the trees or spoor of the animals, but only this dazzling reflection of the great white bird.

He went back for the first time to his people without food. That night he hardly slept. Whether he closed his eyes or opened them, he saw only the reflection of the bird. He thought that by morning he would have done with the bird, but again wherever he hunted this memory of this reflection dazzled his eyes. So it went on day after day. And his people, knowing that something was eating his heart out of him, although they could not put a name to it, tried to show him how they loved him by singing and dancing to him. Yet by day he became more and more silent. He would not eat, he could not sleep and in the air he realised that he would never rest again until he saw the bird itself. His people did everything to persuade him not to go on what seemed so foolish a search. He only said: 'I have seen the reflection of the bird and now

I must find and see the bird itself, but when I have seen it I will return to tell you all.'

He went back into the forest of Duk-A-Duk-Duk. He stayed and watched for days by the pool but the bird did not come back. He went on through the forest, and over the great wasteland plain so far and wide and long that the heart of the bravest who tries to cross it will cry out within: 'Oh! mother. I am lost' and turn back. But he went on and after the desert and through more plain, and forests and valleys; over the months and the years he went among many strange peoples and countries. Everywhere he asked for news of the bird. But everywhere people would either say that they had never heard of such a bird and that it must be a story for old women, or 'Ah, yes, we have heard of someone who once said he had seen such a bird, but we've never seen it ourselves.' At one faraway place indeed there were people who said: 'What a pity you did not come last night, because the bird roosted very nearby here, on its way to the West.' Encouraged for once, he went on searching but still without success until at last he had become a very old man, who had almost lost all memory of the people who had loved him utterly and was feeling only 'now I shall have to die without seeing the bird that once made the blue water white.'

But when he was very, very near the end of his strength, he came to the foot of a very high mountain and met some people who lived around it. When he asked them for news of the bird they said at once: 'Ah yes, we know of the bird. It makes its home on top of the mountain and comes there every night to sleep.'

So, slowly, he started to climb the mountain. After days of climbing, one evening as the sun was just about to set, he came to the bottom of a great cliff that was the top of the mountain. The cliff was as high as it was sheer. He knew he would never be able to climb it – and lay down on the ground ready to die, accepting that he had failed and saying to himself: 'Now I shall never see the bird whose reflection made me look for it for so long.' But as he said that, a voice spoke on this light wind that always comes out of evening and commanded him to look up. He looked. High up in the sky – red as blood with the red of the reddest of red sunsets, he saw a white feather come fluttering down. He held out his hand and, amazed, he felt the feather settling into his trembling

151

fingers. He grasped it firmly with the last of the strength that comes only to the dying, and with this one feather in his hand he died utterly content.

I was always moved by this story in some utterly incomprehensible way and asked my old nurse what the name of the bird was, and in a very sad voice she would say, 'The bird today has many names, for most people have forgotten what it was called in the beginning, but the people of the early race called it the Bird of Truth.'

There, of course, we have the secret of the story, indeed the secret of the meaning of art, why artists are important, because all art is a means of heightening through tension our perception of truth and widening our awareness of reality. And I had to learn very early on that all this unwritten literature always moved on two levels; there was the manifest level where it was an event in everyday reality, but there was another level where within the person who truly took the story inside himself, it acquired a deeper symbolic sort of significance. Take the feather, for instance: the feather is very important here because in a sense it represents the bird and the bird always has been the symbol, the image of what comes inspired, out of the blue, without our wishing it even, into our imagination. And that's why the African chief wears a feather in the band round his head to show that his head is full of inspired wisdom.

What is particularly outstanding and remarkable about this unwritten literature of Africa is how a kind of cosmic awareness comes into the imagination of man and enlarges it by a kind of star consciousness. If you're born, as I was, in this packed starry sky of the southern hemisphere, packed in a way, alas, the northern hemisphere is not, and where at night you can see the stars rising one after the other over the horizon, where you experience star-rise as well as moon-rise and sunrise, you can understand why. Many of the stories that you hear even now in the desert are star stories. They talk of a moment when the stars threw down their spears, literally; the morning star is described again and again as coming home with an arrow in his bow and a spear in his hand. One of the loveliest of all the star stories is of how the Milky Way came to be made: the Milky Way was the creation of a young, lonely, suffering girl of the stone-age people. She was isolated because she was for the first time becoming a woman and she was sour and bitter. As she looked out at the fire outside her hut dying down it was as if she were looking at her childhood, burned out, lying there in front of her. In the deepest moment of her bitterness suddenly she looked up and saw the stars and, reassured, said to herself 'I must join the stars'. She discovered the great secret that, if you can find a meaning in suffering, there is no suffering so great that you cannot endure it, and suddenly she found a meaning in her suffering and she found it in the following way: she went out, picked up the coals that were left in the fire and threw them high into the sky, and as she threw them she addressed the coals thus:

The Milky Way
TRADITIONAL

The wood ashes which are here mixed together have to become utterly the Milky Way. They must lie white along in the sky that the stars may stand outside of their way, so that the Milky Way is utterly the Milky Way. Then the stars, turning back to fetch the break of day, can come to lie nicely beside the Milky Way. The stars become white when the sun comes out. But when the darkness comes, the stars grow red, while the Milky Way becomes white and gently glows, giving a little light for the people so that they who have been caught in the darkness may find their way home in the middle of the night. For the earth would not have been a little light if it had not been for the stars and the Milky Way.

In Africa, as in ancient Greece, the Milky Way is the feminine contribution to life. This great circle of light that goes right round the universe, and in which our solar system spins, is almost a magic circle. Somewhere it protects us as it protected the girl and as it was conveyed in her story. You'll understand why I was so moved one evening in the desert coming home to a little group of stone-age people. And suddenly against the star glimmer, there was no moon, it was very bright, I thought I saw a woman and I stood still and watched and then I saw she was holding up a child of about six weeks old to the stars and she was saying to the stars, 'Oh you who sit up there with your hearts full of light and full of plenty, please give my child also the heart of a star'.

Now what's so amazing in a masculine-dominated world like Africa, where the man has played an even more despotic role than he has in Europe, and that's saying a lot, is that so many of the truest voices to break through the male barrier have been women's voices. Because of the way in which the feminine spirit breaks through into a male-dominated imagination I would like to offer you the story of a noble Abyssinian, an Ethiopian woman who lived nearly nine hundred years ago. It's something to this day which I think if I were a Minister of Education I would make every boy learn by heart.

Introduction to a Science of Mythology
JUNG and KERENYI trans R. F. C. HULL

How can a man know what a woman's life is? A woman's life is quite different from a man's. God ordered it so. A man is the same from the time of his circumcision to the time of his withering. He is the same before he has sought out a woman for the first time, and afterwards. But the day when a woman enjoys her first love cuts her in two. She becomes another woman on that day. The man is the same after his first love as he was before. The woman is from the day of her first love another. That continues all through life. The man spends a night by a woman and goes away. His life and body are always the same. The woman conceives. As a mother she is another person than the woman without child. She carries the fruit of the night nine months long in her body. Something grows. Something grows into her life that never again departs from it. She is a mother. She is and remains a mother even though her child die, though all her children die. For at one time she carried the child under her heart. And it does not go out of her heart ever again. Not even when it is dead. All this the man does not know, he knows nothing. He does not know the difference before love and after love, before motherhood and after motherhood. He can know nothing. Only a woman can know that and speak of that. That is why we won't be told what to do by our husbands. A woman can only do one thing. She can respect herself. She can keep herself decent. She must always be maiden and always be mother. Before every love she is a maiden, after every love she is a mother. In this you can see whether she is a good woman or not.

Reader: Ingaret Giffard

Full Selection:
A Story Like the Wind, LAURENS VAN DER POST
The Story of the Great White Bird, TRADITIONAL
The Lost World of the Kalahari, LAURENS VAN DER POST
The Zebras, ROY CAMPBELL
Ula Masondo's Dream, WILLIAM PLOMER
The Milky Way, TRADITIONAL
Introduction to a Science of Mythology, JUNG and KERENYI trans
   R. F. C. HULL
Daisies in Namaqualand, INGRID JONKER trans WILLIAM PLOMER
The Taste of the Fruit, WILLIAM PLOMER
The Flaming Terrapin, ROY CAMPBELL
Out of Africa, KAREN BLIXEN

DENNIS POTTER

1976

Television as a medium is often derided, and as a radio producer I have not been above taking an occasional swipe at my colleagues who are hooked on small moving pictures. The ratio of bullshit to talent amongst them used to strike me as being a little too weighted in favour of the former, but I suppose the truth is that real talent is rare in any endeavour and radio is not without its share of overweening competence. It is always a pleasure to salute the exceptions: Dennis Potter with his searching, questioning, absorbing plays and serials has for decades set a standard by which television drama in general must find itself judged.

'Tell me what you like,' said Ruskin, 'and I'll tell you what you are.' Hm. Maybe. I am not too keen to be quite so easily locatable as this or that sort of person. Sometimes I want the printed word to console me, sometimes to amuse, or challenge, or even frighten me – so many demands – and then, of course, there are occasions when I get pleasure from the succulent adjectives on the side of a sauce bottle. And, ah! the cornflake packets of yesteryear – red words, green words, blue words filling the void between the spoon, the jug and the sugar bowl. No, you cannot diagnose me by what I have read and liked, only by what I have read and forgotten, or even by what I have read and then eaten.

At the junior school next to the churchyard there was a young woman who taught us six- and seven-year-olds with such sweet grace, and so wondrous a smile, such lovely eyes and such – naturally I fell in love for the very first time. Certain fairy tales at *her* lips were full of mysterious tensions and secrets I had to wait years and years to unravel. Here's an extract from one of Grimms' fairy tales which *almost* tells a child all he wants to know and was too afraid to ask.

Grimms' Fairy Tales

After a couple of years had passed away, it happened that the King's son was riding through the wood, and came by the tower. There he heard a song so beautiful that he stood still and listened. It was Rapunzel, who, to pass the time of her loneliness away, was exercising her sweet voice. The King's son wished to ascend to her, and looked for a door in the tower, but he could not find one.

So he rode home, but the song had touched his heart so much that he went every day to the forest and listened to it, and as he thus stood one day behind a tree, he saw the Witch come up, and heard her call out –

'Rapunzel! Rapunzel! Let down your hair.'

Then Rapunzel let down her long and beautiful tresses, as fine

as spun gold, and the Witch mounted up. 'Is that the ladder on which one must climb? Then I will try my luck too,' said the Prince; and the following day, as he felt quite lonely, he went to the tower, and said –
'Rapunzel! Rapunzel! Let down your hair.'
Then the tresses fell down and he climbed up.

Rapunzel was much frightened at first when a man came in, for she had never seen one before; but the King's son talked in a loving way to her, and told how his heart had been so moved by her singing. So Rapunzel lost her terror, and when he asked if she would have him for a husband, and she saw that he was young and handsome, she thought 'Any one may have me rather than the old woman,' so, saying 'Yes,' she put her hand within his . . .

The old woman found out nothing, until one day Rapunzel innocently said, 'Tell me, mother, how it happens you find it more difficult to come up to me than the young King's son who is with me in a moment!'

'Oh, you wicked child!' exclaimed the Witch; 'I thought I had separated you from all the world, and yet you have deceived me.' And, seizing Rapunzel's hair in a fury, snip, snap, she cut off all her beautiful tresses, and they fell upon the ground. Then she was so hard-hearted that she took the poor maiden into a great desert, and left her to die in great misery and grief.

The old Witch bound the shorn tresses fast above to the window-latch, and when the King's son came, and called out 'Rapunzel! Rapunzel! Let down your hair,' she let them down. The Prince mounted, but when he got to the top he found, not his dear Rapunzel but the Witch, who looked at him with furious and wicked eyes.

'Aha!' she exclaimed scornfully, '– the beautiful bird sits no longer in her nest, singing; the cat has taken her away, and will now scratch out your eyes. To you Rapunzel is lost, you will never see her again.'

The Prince lost his senses with grief at these words, and sprang out of the window of the tower in his bewilderment. His life he escaped with, but the thorns into which he fell put out his eyes. So he wandered, blind, in the forest, eating nothing but berries and roots, and doing nothing but weep and lament for the loss of his dear wife.

He wandered about thus, in great misery, for some few years, and at last arrived at the desert where Rapunzel, with her twins – a boy and a girl – which had been born, lived in great sorrow. Hearing a voice which he thought he knew, he followed in its direction; and, as he approached, Rapunzel recognized him, and fell upon his neck and wept. Two of her tears moistened his eyes, and they became clear again so that he could see as well as ever.

There was a time when I would not have liked to be told that that story came from Germany. I started school in 1940 and so much of my childhood was filled to the brim with the war. My patriotism was total. The villains in the shrunken comics said *Achtung!* and *Himmel!* and *Ach, so-o-o* and *Englander pig-dog!* We, of course, were gentlemen at arms, saints in khaki or airforce blue. A poem by Sir Henry Newbolt – written much earlier, of course – brings back the way a small boy saw the true nature of the struggle. I am still able to enjoy it as dum-di-dum twaddle – and you will surely recognize the opening line.

Vitae Lampada
SIR HENRY NEWBOLT

There's a breathless hush in the Close tonight –
Ten to make and the match to win –
A bumping pitch and a blinding light,
An hour to play and the last man in.
And it's not for the sake of a ribboned coat,
Or the selfish hope of a season's fame,
But his Captain's hand on his shoulder smote –
'Play up! play up! and play the game!'

The sand of the desert is sodden red, –
Red with the wreck of a square that broke; –
The Gatling's jammed and the Colonel dead,
And the Regiment blind with dust and smoke.
The river of death has brimmed his banks,
And England's far, and Honour a name,
But the voice of a schoolboy rallies the ranks:
'Play up! play up! and play the game!'

This is the word that year by year
While in her place the School is set,
Every one of her sons must hear,
And none that hears it dare forget.
This they all with a joyful mind
Bear through life like a torch in flame,
And falling fling to the host behind –
'Play up! play up! and play the game!'

It's occasionally sneaky and diverting, if not very profound, to see conflict between writers, who can of course be exceptionally childish, as I'm often being told, in terms of the yah-boo melodramas of the playground. A few sentences will soon disclose a sanctimonious creep or one who is prepared to put out his tongue. When Wordsworth aloofly referred to William Hazlitt as a 'miscreant' and 'not a proper person to be admitted into respectable society' he was already half-way to providing a picture of a man who warms the heart. Hazlitt was not an easy or comfortable person to know, it seems, and he is still not a comfortable writer to meet on the page. He used himself and used up himself, a formidable essayist, an absolute master of English prose, a writer who set out to mock and scourge all and any examples of humbug, cant and time-serving which crossed his path.

I have great difficulty in choosing a suitable piece from Hazlitt, mostly because he is the writer I revere above all others for the trenchant pertinence of his opinions, for his wit and style and honesty, and for his brave, uncompromising spirit and insights. Hazlitt could quite properly claim that he never wrote a single line which betrayed a principle or disguised a feeling. To read him is to *know* him.

Hazlitt was – and *needed* to be – a master of invective. To show this necessary and exhilarating art at full pitch I have chosen the opening and closing paragraphs of his long open letter to William Gifford in 1819. Gifford was a powerful editor and critic, but a terrible reactionary, using his position to damn all new and liberal voices. He abused the young Keats, for example. Hazlitt went for him, neck and crop. There is no more lethal, and no more justly aimed, invective than this in the English language. This is just a fragment – imagine the rest.

159

A Letter to William Gifford
WILLIAM HAZLITT

Sir, – you have an ugly trick of saying what is not true of anyone you do not like; and it will be the object of this letter to cure you of it. You say what you please of others: It is time you were told what *you* are. In doing this, give me leave to borrow the familiarity of your style: for the fidelity of the picture I shall be answerable.

There cannot be a greater nuisance than a dull, envious, pragmatical, low-bred man, who is placed as you are in the situation of the Editor of such work as the Quarterly Review. Conscious that his reputation stands on very slender and narrow grounds, he is naturally jealous of that of others. He insults over unsuccessful authors; he hates successful ones. He is angry at the faults of a work; more angry at its excellences. If an opinion is old, he treats it with supercilious indifference; if it is new it provokes his rage. He cavils at what he does not comprehend, and misrepresents what he knows to be true. Bound to go through the nauseous task of abusing all those who are not like himself and abject tools of power, his irritation increases with the number of obstacles he encounters, and the number of sacrifices he is obliged to make of commonsense and decency to his interest and self conceit. Every instance of prevarication he wilfully commits makes him more in love with hypocrisy, and every indulgence of his hired malignity makes him more disposed to repeat the insult and injury. Grown old in the service of corruption, he drivels onto the last with prostituted impotence and shameless effrontery; salves a meagre reputation for wit by venting the driblets of his spleen and impertinence on others; answers their arguments by confuting himself; mistakes habitual obtuseness of intellect for a particular acuteness, not to be imposed upon by shallow appearances; unprincipled rancour for zealous loyalty; and the irritable, discontented, vindictive, peevish effusions of bodily pain and mental imbecility for proofs of refinement of taste and strength of understanding.

Such, sir is the picture of which you have sat for the outline.

I sometimes think of that glorious onslaught when I see one of the Post Office advertisements: 'Someone, somewhere, wants a letter from you'. It all depends.

The Diary of a Nobody by George and Weedon Grossmith –
which first appeared in book form in 1892 – is the nicest, happiest,
least malicious satire, and most endearing invention I have ever
read. Time and time again I go back to this fictional diary of dear,
naive Mr Pooter, the city clerk, who resides at The Laurels,
Brickfield Terrace, Holloway, six rooms not counting the base-
ment, ten steps up to the front door and a nice little back garden
that runs down to the railway. 'After my work in the City, I like to
be at home,' writes Mr Pooter. 'What is the good of a home, if you
are never in it?' My sentiments exactly.

Anyway, here we are with Mr Pooter, his paint-pot enthusi-
asms, his dreadful jokes, his wife Carrie and his two friends, Mr
Gowing and Mr Cummings:

The Diary of a Nobody
GEORGE and WEEDON GROSSMITH

April 27 – Painted the bath red, and was delighted with the result.
Sorry to say Carrie was not, in fact, we had a few words about it.
She said I ought to have consulted her, and she had never heard
of such a thing as a bath being painted red. I replied: 'It's merely a
matter of taste.'

Fortunately further argument on the subject was stopped by a
voice saying, 'May I come in?' It was only Cummings, who said,
'Your maid opened the door, and asked me to excuse her showing me in, as she was wringing out some socks.' I was delighted to
see him, and suggested we should have a game of whist with a
dummy, and by way of merriment said: 'You can be the dummy.'
Cummings (I thought rather ill-naturedly) replied: 'Funny as
usual.' He said he couldn't stop, he only called to leave me the
Bicycle News, as he had done with it.

Another ring at the bell; it was Gowing, who said he 'must
apologize for coming so often, and that one of these days we must
come round to him.' I said: 'A very extraordinary thing has struck
me.' 'Something funny, as usual,' said Cummings. 'Yes,' I replied; 'I think even you will say so this time. It's concerning you
both; for doesn't it seem odd that Gowing's always coming and
Cummings always going?' Carrie, who had evidently quite forgotten about the bath, went into fits of laughter, and as for

myself, I fairly doubled up in my chair, till it cracked beneath me. I think this was one of the best jokes I have ever made.

Then imagine my astonishment on perceiving both Cummings and Gowing perfectly silent, and without a smile on their faces. After rather an unpleasant pause, Cummings, who had opened a cigar-case, closed it up again and said, 'Yes – I think, after that, I *shall* be going, and I am sorry I fail to see the fun of your jokes.' Gowing said he didn't mind a joke when it wasn't rude, but a pun on a name, to his thinking, was certainly a little wanting in good taste. Cummings followed up by saying, if it had been said by anyone else but myself, he shouldn't have entered the house again. This rather unpleasantly terminated what might have been a cheerful evening. However, it was as well they went, for the charwoman had finished up the remains of the cold pork.

In conclusion, I want you, please, to listen to the final stretch of Bishop King's, Henry King's, *Exequy* for his dead wife, Anne, who died young in 1624. I *have* to say, though, that I can never read this poem, in my head or out loud, without feeling extremely moved. It is, surely, the most beautiful and moving elegy in our language, in which every rhyme at the end of every line pushes it gradually and inevitably to a consummation in which love finally vanquishes doubt, and calm hope subsumes grief. The poet awaits his own death, seeing each passing minute of his life on this earth as part of the journey towards his dead wife and the reunion beyond the grave when 'I shall at last sit down by Thee'. The power of the feeling and the lucid grace of the resignation, the confidence is such that I am aware when I read this poem, even in the face of bereavement, even in the anguish of doubt, that I am somehow being touched by *some*, at least, some of that inner clarity and faith.

Exequy
HENRY KING

Sleep on my love in thy cold bed
Never to be disquieted!
My last good night! Thou wilt not wake
Till I thy fate shall overtake:

Till age, or grief, or sickness must
Marry my body to that dust
It so much loves; and fill the room
My heart keeps empty in thy tomb.
Stay for me there; I will not fail
To meet thee in that hollow Vale.
And think not much of my delay;
I am already on the way,
And follow thee with all the speed
Desire can make, or sorrows breed.
Each minute is a short degree,
And ev'ry hour a step towards thee,
At night when I betake to rest,
Next Morn I rise nearer my West
Of life almost by eight hours sail,
Than when sleep breath'd his drowsie gale.

'Tis true, with shame and grief I yield,
Thou like the Van first took'st the field,
And gotten hast the victory
In thus adventuring to die
Before me, whose more years might crave
A just precedence in the grave.
But Hark! My pulse like a soft drum
Beats my approach, tells thee I come;
And slow howe'er my marches be,
I shall at last sit down by Thee.

The thought of this bids me go on,
And wait my dissolution
With hope and comfort. Dear (forgive
The crime) I am content to live
Divided, but with half a heart,
Till we shall meet and never part.

I think we should always be willing to be surprised by literature in whatever shell or carapace we inhabit. Words divide us off from all other creatures, but they ought not to be used, wilfully or wantonly, to divide us off from each other. In literature, at least, the atheist can speak to the Christian, and the revolutionary can address the conformist. Good writing seeks completeness, wholeness. Words strongly felt, words properly arranged, scraped out of other people's experiences and insights, *can* complete and nourish and disturb our own lives. Mind you, I don't over-value the emancipations of a liberal culture, and I know that some at least of the guards in the Nazi concentration camps went off duty from the gas chambers and then read Goethe or listened to Beethoven and then went back to work. Our first duty is to the *people*, not the words in front of us, to their hopes and their pains and their needs. If we bow down before narrow ideas, cruel greeds, heartless systems or vacant money machines, then all the great *and* lesser literature, all the great *and* occasional art, will not serve us one jot. The books around us, quiet libraries full of this or that endeavour or humour, even these small pieces this evening, are only open to us if we are open to them. (And never mind the succulent adjectives on the sauce bottle and the cornflake packets of yesteryear!)

Reader: June Barrie

Full selection:
Psalm 35, THE BIBLE
Fairy Tales, THE BROTHERS GRIMM
Vitae Lampada, SIR HENRY NEWBOLT
Just William, RICHMAL CROMPTON
A Letter to William Gifford, WILLIAM HAZLITT
Ivanov, ANTON CHEKHOV
The Wasteland, T. S. ELIOT
The Mayor of Casterbridge, THOMAS HARDY
The Diary of a Nobody, GEORGE and WEEDON GROSSMITH
In Memoriam, ALFRED LORD TENNYSON
The Big Sleep, RAYMOND CHANDLER
Exequy, HENRY KING

FREDERIC RAPHAEL

1978

Several years ago, before this and many of the other programmes included in this volume were produced by the late Brian Patten, I stepped into a lift in Television Centre, my nose buried in Like Men Betrayed, *a novel by Frederic Raphael. 'Good heavens! Are you enjoying it?' came a voice from the other side of the lift. 'Yes, very much,' I said, and then looked up to find myself face to face with the author. Sometimes it's very easy to make someone's day. That was my only meeting to date with Frederic Raphael, although there is a degree of self-mockery in his 'With Great Pleasure' script which makes me think he would be agreeable company. When he talks about poetry he says 'Every prose writer has the uneasy feeling that, compared to a poet, he is a staid married man of lamentably bourgeois provenance who cannot aspire to the daring liberties of the true blade.' He is more waspish, however, on the subject of playwrights: 'It still seems to me that, considering the brevity of their work, they earn their fame and their fortune on singularly easy terms.' Fighting talk!*

I have been working recently on a new translation of the *Oresteia* of Aeschylus, for BBC television. I have had the good fortune to collaborate on this with a good scholar, Kenneth McLeish, and so have been saved from the danger of schoolboy howlers, to which all the years I spent studying the Classics never rendered me wholly immune. But there are other pitfalls for the translator, not least the danger of falling into translationese. A great Classical scholar, A. E. Housman, once wrote the perfect warning to translators, and incidentally one of the best parodies of the language.

A Fragment of a Greek Tragedy
A. E. HOUSMAN

CHORUS: O suitably-attired-in-leather-boots
Head of a traveller, wherefore seeking whom
Whence by what way how purposed art thou come
To this well-nightingaled vicinity?
My object in enquiring is to know.
But if you happen to be deaf and dumb
And do not understand a word I say,
Then wave your hand, to signify as much.

ALCMEON: I journeyed hither a Boeotian road,

CHORUS: Sailing on horseback, or with feet for oars?

ALCMEON: Plying with speed my partnership of legs.

CHORUS: Beneath a shining or a rainy Zeus?

ALCMEON: Mud's sister, not himself, adorns my shoes.

CHORUS: To learn your name would not displease me much.

ALCMEON: Not all that men desire do they obtain.

CHORUS: Might I then hear at what your presence shoots.

ALCMEON: A shepherd's questioned mouth informed me
that—

CHORUS: What? for I know not yet what you will say—

ALCMEON: Nor will you ever, if you interrupt.

CHORUS: Proceed and I will hold my speechless tongue.

ALCMEON: —This house was Eriphyla's, no one's else.

CHORUS: Nor did he shame his throat with hateful lies.

ALCMEON: May I then enter, passing through the door?

CHORUS: Go, chase into the house a lucky foot.
And, O my son, be, on the one hand, good
And do not, on the other hand, be bad;
For that is very much the safest plan.

ALCMEON: I go into the house with heels and speed.

Malcolm Muggeridge is not a man with whom I have any illusions of shared opinions. Nothing that he has said seems to me more wildly silly than his assertion, in a review some years ago, that Lord Byron was the most odious man who ever lived, or words to that effect. I daresay that Professor Wilson Knight was going a bit far when he accused his Lordship of possessing a whole volume full of Christian Virtues, but not even writing two unproduced screenplays on Byron has jaded my affection for the author, and impersonator, of 'Childe Harold' and 'Don Juan' and, above all, the writer of some of the best letters in English. If you can read Byron's correspondence and not warm to the man, I doubt if you have much sense of the comedy of life or taste for vitality.

Here he is writing to his friend Douglas Kinnaird after hearing that the contemporary Lord Longfords and Malcolm Muggeridges had been shocked by the latest section of 'Don Juan'.

Letter to Douglas Kinnaird
LORD BYRON

My dear Douglas – My late expenditure has arisen from living at a distance from Venice and being obliged to keep up two establishments, from frequent journeys – and buying some furniture and books as well as a horse or two – and not from any renewal of the EPICUREAN system as you suspect. I have been faithful to my honest liaison with Countess Guiccioli – and I can assure you that *She* has never cost me directly or indirectly a sixpence – indeed the circumstances of herself and family render this no merit. – I never offered her but one present – a broach of brilliants – and she sent it back to me with her *own hair* in it (I shall *not* say of *what part* but *that* is an Italian custom) and a note to say that she was not in the habit of receiving presents of that value – but hoped I would not consider her sending it back as an affront – nor the value diminished by the enclosure. – I have not had a whore this half-year – confining myself to the strictest adultery. – Why should you prevent Hanson from making a *peer* if he likes it – I think the '*Garretting*' would be by far the best parliamentary privilege – I know of. – Damn your delicacy. – It is a low commercial quality – and very unworthy a man who prefixes 'honourable' to his nomenclature. If you say I must sign the bonds – I suppose that I must – but it is very iniquitous to make me pay my debts – you have no idea of the pain it gives one. – Pray do three things – get my property out of the *funds* – get Rochdale sold – get me some information from Perry about *South America* – and 4thly ask Lady Noel not to live so very long. – As to Subscribing to Manchester –

if I do that – I will write a letter to Burdett – for publication – to accompany the Subscription – which shall be more radical than anything yet rooted – but I feel lazy. – I have thought of this for some time – but alas! the air of this accursed Italy enervates – and disenfranchises the thoughts of a man after nearly four years of respiration – to say nothing of emission. – As to 'Don Juan' – confess – confess you dog – and be candid – that it is the sublime of *that there* sort of writing – it may be bawdy – but is it not good English? – it may be profligate – but is it not *life*, is it not *the thing*? – Could any man have written it – who has not lived in the world? – and tooled in a post-chaise? in a hackney coach? in a Gondola? against a wall? in a court carriage? in a vis à vis? – on a table – and under it? – I have written about a hundred stanzas of a third Canto – but it is damned modest – the outcry has frightened me.

There are some kinds of literary art and subject matter which require, somehow, the certificate of experience. Siegfried Sassoon's war poems are rendered unanswerable in their ferocious disgust by our knowledge that Sassoon himself endured the hell of the front line. His gallantry was as remarkable as the dandyism which led him, after a display of courage that won him the MC, to sit in a captured trench reading a volume of poetry. Had Sassoon denounced the war from the comfort of a library, his poem *The General* would have been, perhaps, no more than a clever exercise in irony. As it is, the cold shivers which Housman associated with true poetry never fail to prickle on my neck when I hear these lines.

The General
SIEGFRIED SASSOON

'Good-morning; good-morning!' the General said
When we met him last week on our way to the line.
Now the soldiers he smiled at are most of 'em dead,
And we're cursing his staff for incompetent swine.
'He's a cheery old card,' grunted Harry to Jack
As they slogged up to Arras with rifle and pack.
. . .
But he did for them both with his plan of attack.

Anthologies have a way of being mock-modest. There is something shameful about confessing that one sometimes uses one's mirror in order to look at, even admire, onself. As if mirrors would be as popular as they are if one could never glimpse oneself in them! I confess therefore with a sort of hangdog shamelessness that I am not above looking at my own work from time to time. Sometimes one wishes that one had not used a certain idea or experience, since one could manage it so much better now, but sometimes one is agreeably surprised to find that the memory of a given passage is less flattering than the text seems, on fresh inspection, to warrant. Forgive me then, as I have already decided to forgive myself, if to end with I choose a passage from a novel of mine, *Like Men Betrayed*, a novel of, I confess, a certain measured sobriety and of which one critic was cruelly kind enough to say that it showed not the smallest glimmer of a sense of humour. In a world where entertainment at all costs is what is so often demanded of writers, it gives me a certain pained pleasure to think that at least once I have been taken for one of those unsmiling souls to whom levity can never be attributed. Here, from that book, is a description of a Greek dance.

Like Men Betrayed
FREDERIC RAPHAEL

Artemis danced as lightly as the sea which makes curtains of sand in gentle scollops along the shore. His feet fretted the sand in the circle and invented nothing. He moved as regularly as the scansion of an old metre, each line and each caesura in its place. He danced with his hands held up, like a puppeteer, and drew the eyes of the others after him. . . .

He took Dmitri by the hands and drew him to his feet. Dmitri, clumsy Dmitri, whose whole life would be perhaps a parody of elegance to hide his disquiet at this kind of direct and physical challenge, he came up like a deck-chair in the hands of a child, falling this way and that in stilted commotion, until Artemis . . . controlled him and, offering him the end of a strangled napkin, drew him into silent conversation. They turned and rode on the swollen sand, turned inside and under each other and Artemis schooled Dmitri in elegance with a mastery the other might find more unforgivable than violence. He could match violence with power, but there was no matching this slim and humorous pedantry. Kesta began to hum and moan like a wire in the wind, the first promise of the storm, while Dmitri was exhausted by the soft precision expected from him. He gasped as if he were dodging walls, as if a court was tight about the dancing pair, tighter than the loose circle of sand, and some penalty was due if one touched the cold face of it.

Artemis defined Dmitri for Katerina that night. He defined the man's limits in front of the girl. He defined his own superiority and he abdicated his share of the world of Stratis and his thick millions. He danced Dmitri as a man and a partner might run down and bewilder a bull with alternate goads. Katerina was his partner, but a partner promised a separation. Artemis allowed Dmitri every chance to command the steps. He bowed and yielded, as a lover will sometimes hesitate in a caress to allow its rejection or will lie back and give his partner the chance to discover the frontier of her own temerity, to assault herself with his body, but Dmitri could only guffaw at such times and make a gross imitation of some grand gesture which he knew to be beyond him. . . . Now Dmitri drew Michael Shaw to his feet, glad to find someone incapable even of parody. And then Artemis was cruel; he broke the chain and left the two to confont the music alone. They stammered and Kosta laughed and raised the rhythm to double and quadruple time till there was something savage in his fingers, something indifferent and immodest. He flung down the last phrases like an insult and clapped his hand over the mouth of his guitar. And then Artemis was like a ghost. As they looked he was dancing again, but beyond them now, down by the sea, he was dancing with the sea, he was measuring himself against the sea, stepping on its skirt as it sipped the land, courting the sea as he had courted Katerina, so that finally she ran to him and the others smiled.

Readers: Angela Down, Norman Rodway

Full Selection:
Cakes and Ale, SOMERSET MAUGHAM

DR ROBERT RUNCIE

1986

Many important people like to surround themselves with the trappings of power – people rushing around after them, an expectation of lavish hospitality, that sort of thing. This Archbishop of Canterbury could hardly have been more different. He clearly did not want any BBC 'brass' in attendance (some would argue that that displayed no more than good sense!) nor did he wish to be especially well fed. He arrived in Broadcasting House reception accompanied only by a couple of close colleagues and joined the production team for sandwiches after the recording. In between *he was delighted and flattered to be sharing a platform with Michael Hordern and Judi Dench.*

I have always enjoyed and envied *style*, not in the sense of high-flown sentiments and ornate wording, but style meaning a directness and sincerity of expression so that the writers convey to my mind as exactly as possible what they are feeling and saying. The following passage expresses what I feel about style with a light but sure touch. It is by Ernest Gowers. He was editor of the *Oxford English Dictionary*, so he should know what he is talking about here.

Plain Words
ERNEST GOWERS

Why do so many writers prefer 'pudder' to simplicity? It seems to be a morbid condition contracted in early manhood. Children show no signs of it. Here, for example, is the response of a child of ten to an invitation to write an essay (its genuineness is guaranteed) on a beast and a bird:

'The bird that I am going to write about is the owl. The owl cannot see at all by day and at night is as blind as a bat.

I do not know much about the owl, so I will go on to the beast which I am to choose. It is the cow. The cow is a mammal. It has six sides – right, left, an upper and below. At the back it has a tail on which hangs a brush. With this it sends the flies away so that they do not fall into the milk. The head is for the purpose of growing horns and so that the mouth can be somewhere. The horns are to butt with, and the mouth is to moo with. Under the cow hangs the milk. It is arranged for milking. When people milk, the milk comes and there is never an end to the supply. How the cow does it I have not yet realised, but it makes more and more. The cow has a fine sense of smell; one can smell it far away. This is the reason for the fresh air in the country.

The man cow is called an ox. It is not a mammal. The cow does not eat much, but what it eats it eats twice, so that it gets enough. When it is hungry it moos, and when it says nothing it is because its inside is all full up with grass.'

My mother was a hairdresser on an ocean liner. I was brought up beside the Mersey in cosmopolitan Liverpool. Perhaps this accounts a little for my lifelong enjoyment of travel. And it is partly just being Scots. The Scots and the Greeks have always gone out into all lands. They have thrived on doing so. But they never forget their native and beloved hills.

I have travelled for its own sake, but far more for the appreciation of other people, and of natural beauty – and for the contemplation of works of Art.

Providence has been very kind to me: allowing me to visit, and learn to love, so many places – Samarkand and San Francisco, Delhi, Venice and Istanbul. All this grew out of my first love for the Greek world. It is to Greece first of all that I long to return.

To celebrate this I have chosen the first three stanzas of Lord Byron's poem 'The Isles of Greece'. This was really nationalist propaganda when Greece was struggling for independence in the 1820s, but it breathes an eternal spirit.

The Isles of Greece
LORD BYRON

The isles of Greece! the isles of Greece
Where burning Sappho loved and sung,
Where grew the arts of war and peace,
Where Delos rose, and Phoebus sprung!
Eternal summer gilds them yet,
But all, except their sun, is set.

The Scian and the Teian muse,
The hero's harp, the lover's lute,
Have found the fame your shores refuse:
Their place of birth alone is mute
To sounds which echo further west
Than your sires' 'Islands of the Blest'.

The mountains look on Marathon –
And Marathon looks on the sea;
And musing there an hour alone,
I dream'd that Greece might still be free;
For standing on the Persian's grave,
I could not deem myself a slave.

When the clouds gather, I frequently turn to that worldly cleric, Sydney Smith. A conservative in religion, and a liberal in politics, he said that his life was like a razor – spent either in hot water or a scrape.

When I have to go to, and possibly speak at, a City dinner, I arm myself with the *Sayings of Sydney Smith*. He is so eminently quotable. He said of someone that their idea of heaven is that of eating pâté de fois gras to the sound of trumpets. I have a Swiss sister-in-law, and I tease her by repeating his remark that Switzerland is an inferior sort of Scotland. Then, who else would have said: 'I have only one illusion left and that is the Archbishop of Canterbury'?

He may now be better known for his bons mots than for his pastoral diligence, but there was that side of him too. The best of both can be found in this letter to Lady Morpeth, who had complained of low spirits. Like many funny people he suffered from melancholy himself.

Letter to Lady Georgiana Morpeth
SYDNEY SMITH

Dear Georgiana,
Nobody has suffered more from low spirits than I have done, so I feel for you.

1. Live as well and drink as much wine as you dare.
2. Go into the shower bath with a small quantity of water at a temperature low enough to give you a slight sensation of cold – 75 or 80 degrees.
3. Amusing books.
4. Short views of human life not further than dinner or tea.
5. Be as busy as you can.
6. See as much as you can of those friends who respect and like you;
7. and of those acquaintances who amuse you.
8. Make no secret of low spirits to your friends but talk of them fully: they are always the worse for dignified concealment.
9. Attend to the effects tea and coffee produce upon you.
10. Compare your lot with that of other people.
11. Don't expect too much of human life, a sorry business at best.
12. Avoid poetry, dramatic representations (except comedy),

music, serious novels, melancholy sentimental people, and everything likely to excite feeling or emotion not ending in active benevolence.

13. Do good and endeavour to please everybody of every degree.
14. Be as much as you can in the open air without fatigue.
15. Make the room where you commonly sit gay and pleasant.
16. Struggle by little and little against idleness.
17. Don't be too severe upon yourself, or underrate yourself, but do yourself justice.
18. Keep good blazing fires.
19. Be firm and constant in the exercise of rational religion.
20. Believe me dear Lady Georgiana very truly yours, Sydney Smith.

I usually only spend working weekends, and any holidays I ever have, at Canterbury. Otherwise, unless overseas, I am at Lambeth. I love Lambeth, for there so much history encircles such a great volume of work being done to service the worldwide Anglican Church of the present. But I love the setting also. Although my vantage point is not quite the same as Wordsworth's, only a few hundred yards separate it from Westminster Bridge. What he wrote in 1802 was entirely true for me this morning.

Upon Westminster Bridge
WILLIAM WORDSWORTH

Earth has not anything to show more fair:
Dull would he be of soul who could pass by
A sight so touching in its majesty:
This City now doth, like a garment, wear
The beauty of the morning; silent, bare,
Ships, towers, domes, theatres, and temples lie
Open unto the fields, and to the sky;
All bright and glittering in the smokeless air.
Never did sun more beautifully steep
In his first splendour, valley, rock or hill;
Ne'er saw I, never felt, a calm so deep!
The river glideth at his own sweet will:
Dear God! the very houses seem asleep;
And all that mighty heart is lying still!

Who am I? Perhaps my selection has revealed parts of an answer that I do not entirely know myself.

Dietrich Boenhoeffer was a German pastor who died in a Nazi prison. He was one of the great prophetic voices of modern times. He saw Christianity in a new kind of balance – relying less on words and more on practical love. Here is his poem about identity. It speaks to my condition. For we do all worry about our identity, and the truth – for Boenhoeffer and for me – is that without God there is no answer.

Who Am I?
DIETRICH BOENHOEFFER

Who am I? They often tell me
I would step from my cell's confinement
calmly, cheerfully, firmly,
like a squire from his country-house.

Who am I? They often tell me
I would talk to my warders
freely and friendly and clearly,
as though it were mine to command.

Who am I? They also tell me
I would bear the days of misfortune
equably, smilingly, proudly,
like one accustomed to win.

Am I then really all that which other men tell of?
Or am I only what I know of myself,
restless and longing and sick, like a bird in a cage,
struggling for breath, as though hands were compressing
my throat,
yearning for colour, for flowers, for the voices of birds,
thirsting for words of kindness, for neighbourliness,
trembling with anger at despotisms and petty humiliation,
tossing in expectation of great events,
powerlessly trembling for friends at an infinite distance,
weary and empty at praying, at thinking, at making,
faint, and ready to say farewell to it all?

Who am I? This or the other?
Am I one person today, and tomorrow another?
Am I both at once? A hypocrite before others,
And before myself a contemptibly woebegone weakling?
Or is it something within me still like a beaten army,
fleeing in disorder from victory already achieved?

Who am I? They mock me, these lonely questions of mine.
Whoever I am, thou knowest, O God, I am thine.

Readers: Michael Hordern, Judi Dench

Full Selection:
Plain Words, ERNEST GOWERS
Lochinvar, SIR WALTER SCOTT
The Merchant of Venice, WILLIAM SHAKESPEARE
The Question, ALEXANDER McKEE
Portraits of Places 1883, HENRY JAMES
Kneeling, R. S. THOMAS
The Strangers All Are Gone, ANTHONY POWELL
The Isles of Greece, LORD BYRON
The Story of Art, E. H. GOMBRICH
Ithaka, C. P. CAVAFY
Thursday, Christmas Eve, KILVERT
Letter to Lady Georgiana Morpeth, SYDNEY SMITH
In a Bath Teashop, JOHN BETJEMAN
Murder in the Cathedral, T. S. ELIOT
Upon Westminster Bridge, WILLIAM WORDSWORTH
Limbo, ALDOUS HUXLEY
Missed, P. G. WODEHOUSE
Who Am I?, DIETRICH BOENHOEFFER
Vision, DAME JULIAN OF NORWICH

JOHN TIMPSON

1986

*The first thing John Timpson said when asked to present an edition of
'With Great Pleasure' was 'Has Redhead done one?' He looked absolutely
delighted when I told him that he had not. Their double act on the 'Today'
programme made the early mornings just bearable. Latterly Timpson's
chairing of 'Any Questions' was entertaining not just for his firm
handling of the panellists, but for his lengthy and witty introductions to
them. He left both jobs earlier than he need to spend more time in his
beloved Norfolk.*

I suppose like many others of my generation, my first encounter
with Literature – with a capital L – was the incomparable, and
to most ten-year-olds quite incomprehensible, William
Shakespeare. I had to learn all the standard speeches, I understood perhaps one line in three, and I'm not sure I understand
them all now, but I find I can still render 'Once more unto the
breach' and 'All the world's a stage' and 'Tomorrow and tomorrow and tomorrow' – I can still get right through to the last
couplet without a falter, even though I often can't remember the
names of people I met yesterday. Perhaps it's because we had
a headmaster who insisted that we actually performed
Shakespeare as well as just reciting it – something which I see has
just been hailed as a breakthrough in modern teaching methods,
but he did it mainly to get publicity. He liked to impress prospective parents by staging entertainments in the Speech Room at
Harrow School – how he acquired the use of it I shall never know,

because the only connection between Harrow School and our school in Harrow was the name of the borough – but of course the parents loved it.

My favourite role was the Duke of Clarence in *Richard III*, who was foully murdered in the Tower. It's the scene with the classic stage direction: 'Enter two murderers', and I remember dying magnificently centre stage as the second murderer cried 'Take that and that, and if that will not do, I'll drown you in the malmsey butt within.' It was great stuff and we hammed it up disgracefully – particularly Clarence's gruesome description of the nightmare he'd had before the murderers appeared.

Richard III
WILLIAM SHAKESPEARE

Methought that I had broken from the Tower,
And was embark'd to cross to Burgundy;
And in my company my brother Gloster;
Who from my cabin tempted me to walk
Upon the hatches: thence we look'd toward England,
And cited up a thousand heavy times,
During the wars of York and Lancaster,
That had befall'n us. As we pac'd along
Upon the giddy footing of the hatches,
Methought that Gloster stumbled; and, in falling,
Struck me, that thought to say him, overboard,
Into the tumbling billows of the main.
Lord, Lord! methought what pain it was to drown:
What dreadful noise of water in mine ears!
What sights of ugly death within mine eyes!
Methought I saw a thousand fearful wrecks;
A thousand men that fishes gnaw'd upon;
Wedges of gold, great anchors, heaps of pearl,
Inestimable stones, unvalu'd jewels,
All scattered in the bottom of the sea:
Some lay in dead men's skulls; and in those holes
Where eyes did once inhabit there were crept,
As 'twere in scorn of eyes, reflecting gems,
That woo'd the slimy bottom of the deep,
And mock'd the dead bones that lay scatter'd by.

But then, my dream was lengthen'd after life;
O, then began the tempest to my soul.
I pass'd, methought, the melancholy flood
With that grim ferryman which poets write of,
Unto the kingdom of perpetual night.
The first that there did greet my stranger soul
Was my great father-in-law, renowned Warwick;
Who cried aloud, 'What scourge for perjury
Can this dark monarchy afford false Clarence?'
And so he vanish'd: then came wandering by
A shadow like an angel, with bright hair
Dabbled in blood; and he shriek'd out aloud,
'Clarence is come, – false, fleeting, perjured Clarence,
That stabb'd me in the field by Tewkesbury; –
Seize on him! Furies, take him unto torment!'
With that, methought, a legion of foul fiends
Environ'd me, and howled in mine ears
Such hideous cries that, with the very noise,
I trembling wak'd, and for a season after
Could not believe but that I was in hell,
Such terrible impression made my dream.

I always look forward to getting back to those vast Norfolk skies and the rolling countryside which is not at all flat and boring as people think – we just say it is to discourage too many visitors, much assisted in that by the vagaries of the Eastern Region of British Rail and the inadequacies of the main roads. I often think it is no accident that the only motorway in East Anglia stops at Cambridge. The other special feature of Norfolk is of course the churches. John Betjeman loved Norfolk too – he called it one of the great architectural treasures of Europe because of the sheer profusion of country churches. Perhaps indeed they are too profuse – our own rector has seven churches to cope with, and that is by no means unusual. Betjeman published a little collection of his poems which may well have been inspired by those Norfolk churches. Here's one I know will appeal to all parsons, including our own.

Blame the Vicar
JOHN BETJEMAN

When things go wrong it's rather tame
To find we are ourselves to blame,
It gets the trouble over quicker
To go and blame things on the Vicar.
The Vicar, after all, is paid
To keep us bright and undismayed.
The Vicar is more virtuous too
Than lay folks such as me and you.
He never swears, he never drinks,
He never *should* say what he thinks.
His collar is the wrong way round,
And that is why he's simply bound
To be the sort of person who
Has nothing very much to do
But take the blame for what goes wrong
And sing in tune at Evensong.
    For what's a Vicar really for
Except to cheer us up? What's more,
He shouldn't ever, ever tell
If there is such a place as Hell,
For if there is it's certain he
Will go to it as well as we.
The Vicar should be all pretence
And never, never give offence.
To preach on Sunday is his task
And lend his mower when we ask
And organise our village fêtes
And sing at Christmas with the waits
And in his car to give us lifts
And when we quarrel, heal the rifts.
To keep his family alive
He should industriously strive
In that enormous house he gets,
And he should always pay his debts,
For he has quite six pounds a week,

And when we're rude he should be meek
And always turn the other cheek.
He should be neat and nicely dressed
With polished shoes and trousers pressed,
For we look up to him as higher
Than anyone, except the Squire.
    Dear People, who have read so far,
I know how really kind you are,
I hope that you are always seeing
Your Vicar as a human being,
Making allowances when he
Does things with which you don't agree.
But there are lots of people who
Are not so kind to him as you.
So in conclusion you shall hear
About a parish somewhere near,
Perhaps your own or maybe not,
And of the Vicars that it got.
    One parson came and people said,
'Alas! Our former Vicar's dead!
And this new man is far more "Low"
Than dear old Reverend so-and-so,
And far too earnest in his preaching,
We do not really like his teaching,
He seems to think we're simply fools
Who've never been to Sunday Schools.'
That Vicar left and by and by
A new one came, 'He's much too "High",'
The people said, 'too like a saint,
His incense makes our Mavis faint.'
So now he's left and they're alone
Without a Vicar of their own.
The living's been amalgamated
With the one next door they've always hated.
    Dear readers, from this rhyme take warning,
And if you heard the bell this morning
Your Vicar went to pray for you,
A task the Prayer Book bids him do.
'Highness' or 'Lowness' do not matter,

You are the Church and must not scatter,
Cling to the Sacraments and pray
And God be with you every day.

For many years now we have had hanging up in our kitchen what I've always known as *The Old Nun's Prayer*, though there are various sources. It includes for instance the word 'Cocksureness' which you do not immediately associate with old nuns. But it's a prayer which combines humility with humour – the sort of thing Rabbi Lionel Blue would probably wish he'd written. It was this prayer that I suggested when I was asked a few years ago to contribute to an anthology called *A Way With Words*, in aid of sufferers from dysphasia, that very distressing disorder which affects the ability to utter and understand language. Many people whose careers and livelihoods depend on that contributed to the book. *The Old Nun's Prayer* does too, but not under my name – under Mrs Thatcher's. She too selected it, and it was only fitting that I should withdraw in her favour. We in the BBC are like that. But at least I can choose it now – and perhaps you'll see why it's an appropriate prayer, not just for Mrs Thatcher but for almost any politician.

An Old English Nun's Prayer

Lord, Thou knowest better than I know myself that I am growing older and will some day be old. Keep me from the fatal habit of thinking I must say something on every subject and on every occasion.

Release me from craving to straighten out everybody's affairs. Make me thoughtful but not moody; helpful but not bossy. With my vast store of wisdom, it seems a pity not to use it all, but Thou knowest Lord that I want a few friends at the end.

Keep my mind from the recital of endless details; give me wings to get to the point. Seal my lips on aches and pains. They are increasing, and love of rehearsing them is becoming sweeter as the years go by. I dare not ask for grace enough to enjoy the tales of other's pains, but help me to endure them with patience.

I dare not ask for improved memory, but for a growing humility and a lessening cocksureness when my memory seems to clash with the memories of others. Teach me the glorious lesson that occasionally I may be mistaken.

Keep me reasonably sweet. I do not want to be a Saint – some of them are so hard to live with – but a sour old person is one of the crowning works of the devil. Give me the ability to see good things in unexpected places and talents in unexpected people. And give me, O Lord, the grace to tell them so.

AMEN

I particularly like that line 'Teach me that occasionally I can be mistaken.' I am sure Mrs Thatcher does too.

I mentioned that I withdrew my claim to that contribution and I had to find another in rather a hurry. As always on such occasions, the mind went blank. But it so happened I was browsing through the *Radio Times* – mainly to see if I'm still working next week – when I came upon a little verse by Leo Marks that has haunted me ever since. There is a romantic and moving story behind the verse, involving a wartime woman agent and a secret code – I won't go into it all because for me this little verse has a life of its own – it doesn't need a background or an explanation. It says in a few simple lines what I think many a husband would like to say to his wife, but after, say, thirty-five years of married life he might think it would sound too sloppy, unless it was some special occasion. Well, this for me is a special occasion.

Code Poem for the French Resistance
LEO MARKS

The life that I have is all that I have,
And the life that I have is yours.
The love that I have of the life that I have
Is yours and yours and yours.

A sleep I shall have
A rest I shall have,
Yet death will be but a pause,
For the peace of my years in the long green grass
Will be yours and yours and yours.

Readers: Carol Drinkwater, Anthony Hyde

Full Selection:
Richard III, WILLIAM SHAKESPEARE
William the Bad, RICHMAL CROMPTON
The Quiet American, GRAHAM GREENE
The Pickwick Papers, CHARLES DICKENS
Scoop, EVELYN WAUGH
The Boy John, SIDNEY GRAPES
Blame the Vicar, JOHN BETJEMAN
Ballad of the Bread Man, CHARLES CAUSLEY
An Old English Nun's Prayer, ANON
Code Poem for the French Resistance, LEO MARKS

SUE TOWNSEND

1987

'Daddy, what's a French letter?' Those words uttered by my ten-year-old son within the confines of St David's Cathedral created a degree of head-turning amongst the tour guide's disciples. 'I'll tell you in a minute,' I whispered, I hoped not too audibly, as I steered him tactfully behind a pillar. After a moment or two of perhaps overly detailed explanation he muttered firmly and a little bored 'You mean a condom?' 'Yes, I suppose I do,' I said. 'By the way, where did you hear the expression "French letter"? You don't hear it so often nowadays.' 'Oh,' he said, 'Adrian Mole.' After that there was nothing for it but to invite Sue Townsend on to the programme. She proved to be a funny, scatty and warm person who was clearly loved by the audience made up of her many friends in Leicester where she lives.

185

Jane Eyre was the first book I read all the way through in one go. I didn't sleep at all. The birds started to sing; I read on. I washed with the book leaning against the taps. I walked to school still reading. I read in Maths and French and in the cloakroom. This extract describes a visit from Mr Brocklehurst, a clergyman who is Superintendent at Lowood School where Jane Eyre was sent when she was eight years old.

Jane Eyre
CHARLOTTE BRONTË

'Miss Temple, Miss Temple, what – *what* is that girl with curled hair? Red hair, ma'am, curled – curled all over?' And extending his cane he pointed to the awful object, his hand shaking as he did so.

'It is Julia Severn,' replied Miss Temple very quietly.

'Julia Severn, ma'am! And why has she, or any other, curled hair? Why, in defiance of every precept and principle of this house, does she conform to the world so openly – here in an evangelical, charitable establishment – as to wear her hair one mass of curls?'

'Julia's hair curls naturally,' returned Miss Temple still more quietly.

'Naturally! Yes, but we are not to conform to nature. I wish these girls to be the children of Grace: and why that abundance? I have again and again intimated that I desire the hair to be arranged closely, modestly, plainly. Miss Temple, that girl's hair must be cut off entirely; I will send a barber tomorrow: and I see others who have far too much of that excrescence – that tall girl, tell her to turn round. Tell all the first form to rise up and direct their faces to the wall.'

Miss Temple passed her handkerchief over her lips, as if to smooth away the involuntary smile that curled them; she gave the order, however, and when the first class could take in what was required of them, they obeyed. Leaning a little back on my bench, I could see the looks and grimaces with which they commented on this manoeuvre: it was a pity Mr Brocklehurst could not see them too; he would perhaps have felt that, whatever he might do with the outside of the cup and platter, the inside was farther beyond his interference than he imagined.

He scrutinised the reverse of these living medals some five minutes, then pronounced sentence. These words fell like the knell of doom.

'All these top-knots must be cut off.'

Miss Temple seemed to remonstrate.

'Madam,' he pursued, 'I have a Master to serve whose kingdom is not of this world: my mission is to mortify in these girls the lusts of the flesh, to teach them to clothe themselves with shamefacedness and sobriety, not with braided hair and costly apparel; and each of the young persons before us has a string of hair twisted in plaits which vanity itself might have woven: these, I repeat, must be cut off.'

One of my many jobs, before I started writing for a living, was as a community warden in two tower blocks that had been filled up with retired people. I soon realized that the pathetic image that old people had was completely misleading. These are Percy Collins' words, he is real and he is seventy-six.

The People of Providence
TONY PARKER

A nice woman my own age, an hour or two in bed together with someone like that, that's always been the thing for me. And so long as it's regular, once a week or so, I'm perfectly content. It doesn't have to be what they call the full thing every time either – I enjoy the love-making and kissing and cuddling as much, or more even sometimes, on its own.

I've never been with a prostitute. I don't somehow fancy that, it's got to be someone I know and like. There again you see I've been lucky, there's any number of ladies around who're my age, widows or single most of them: I don't think it's right to run the risk of perhaps someone's husband finding out and making trouble about it. Most of them seem to feel the same way I do. I usually say something like 'Well shall we try it and see how it goes, and if you don't like it we'll not go on with it.' But there's not many that don't. I think there's something about sex that's really nice, it's fun but it's more than that, it gives you a good warm feeling inside of you, you're being absolutely natural. It's giving somebody pleasure, it's you giving somebody pleasure. I think that's very nice and very good. So long as you don't get jealous about them and they don't get jealous about you, it's not doing harm to anyone as far as I can see.

I suppose there must be about twelve or so ladies that we're on that kind of terms together. Most of them like myself belong to the church – it's a good meeting place to come into contact with other people who're on their own. And if someone goes to church you know she's got what you call a level-headed approach to things; she's not going to be like somebody you might pick up casually in a pub. I don't like the sort of coarse jokes you sometimes hear women making in pubs. If I'm love-making with someone I prefer her to be a conventional sort of person like myself.

Sojourner Truth was a freed slave who travelled around the United States trying to free her people from slavery. She believed in equality for all, black and white and women with men. At one meeting where she was due to speak some clergymen said that women could never be equal because men had more intelligence, because Christ was a man and because of the sin of Eve. She made the following speech.

Ain't I a Woman?
SOJOURNER TRUTH

Well, children, where there is so much racket there must be something out of kilter. I think that 'twixt the negroes of the South and women of the North, all talking about rights, the white men will be in a fix pretty soon. But what's all this here talking about?

That man over there says that women need to be helped into carriages, and lifted over ditches, and to have the best place everywhere. Nobody ever helps me into carriages, or over mud-puddles, or gives me any best place! And ain't I a woman? Look at me! Look at my arm! I have ploughed and planted, and gathered into barns, and no man could head me! And ain't I a woman? I could work as much and eat as much as a man – when I could get it – and bear the lash as well! And ain't I a woman? I have borne thirteen children; and seen them most all sold off to slavery, and when I cried out with my mother's grief, none but Jesus heard me! And ain't I a woman?

Then they talk about this thing in the head; what's this they call it? (Intellect, someone whispers.) That's it, honey. What's that got to do with women's rights or negro's rights? If my cup won't hold but a pint, and yours holds a quart, wouldn't you be mean not to let me have my little half-measure full?

Then that little black man in black there, he says women can't have as much rights as men, 'cause Christ wasn't a woman! Where did your Christ come from? Where did your Christ come from? From God and a woman! Man had nothing to do with Him!

If the first woman God ever made was strong enough to turn the world upside down all alone, these women together ought to be able to turn it back, and get it right-side up again! And now they is asking to do it, the men better let them.

Obliged to you for hearing me, and now Old Sojourner ain't got nothing more to say.

Wouldn't you love to hear a politician tell the truth? Just once? The following letter is a guess at how the truth might sound from one particular politician.

Dear Mr Eggnogge
THE *SPITTING IMAGE* BOOK 1987

Dear Ernest Eggnogge,
I've received some whining, snivelling, wipe my eyes, pass the Kleenex letters in my time, but yours truly takes the Huntley and Palmers. Quite frankly I don't give a toss that your old mother died of hypothermia last winter or that your zit-faced moronic teenaged lout of a son has not worked since leaving school. And the news that your wife has been waiting for six years to have her nasty infected womb removed left me cold. Haven't you got a sharp knife for God's sake?

You dare to say that I am 'out of touch with real people' and suggest I 'jump on a train and come up North'.

Firstly, Mr Eggnogge, I am married to a 'real person'. Secondly, I would rather spend the night with Guy the Gorilla (Yes, I know he's dead) than climb aboard one of those vile rattling contraptions and visit you all up there in slag heap land. We have nothing in common. I hate ferrets, dripping, pigeons, corner shops and fat, ugly, pale people who are unable to speak in complete sentences and who don't understand how the International Monetary Fund works.

Finally, at the end of your letter you bleat on about your dole payment calling it 'a pittance' and 'an affront to your dignity'. This last bit made me laugh quite a lot. What did you get for Christmas? A subscription to *New Society*?

Listen parasite, that's the point, don't you see? We don't need you and your sort anymore – get the message now? Take my advice, shovel the coal out of the bath, then fill it up and jump in and drown yourself.

(NB Note to private secretary: Tidy this up a bit will you?)

And this is the tidied up version that Ernest Eggnogge actually received:

Dear Mr Eggnogge,
The Prime Minister was most concerned to hear of your difficulties. She is looking into the various matters you raised in your letter.
Yours sincerely
Rupert Brown-Bear

I think we accept too meekly the rules that professional politicians lay down for us. They are no wiser than you or I. When the Nazi storm troopers first goose-stepped through Berlin the German people should have laughed them off the streets. Laughter can be a very powerful weapon. Though there comes a time when even laughter fails.

This was written by Pastor Niemoeller, who was a prisoner of the Nazis.

First They Came for the Jews
PASTOR NIEMOELLER

First they came for the Jews
And I did not speak out –
Because I was not a Jew.

Then they came for the Communists
And I did not speak out –
Because I was not a Communist.

Then they came for the Trade
Unionists and I did not speak out –
Because I was not a Trade Unionist.

Then they came for me –
And there was no one left
To speak out for me.

Readers: Peter Jeffrey, Julia Hills

Full Selection:
Janet and John, MABEL O'DONNELL and RONA MUNRO
Just William's Luck, RICHMAL CROMPTON
Jane Eyre, CHARLOTTE BRONTË
Cargoes, JOHN MASEFIELD
Lucky Jim, KINGSLEY AMIS
Songs For a Coloured Singer, ELIZABETH BISHOP
Extracts from Punch *and* Country Life
The People of Providence, TONY PARKER
Consult Me For All You Want To Know,
    FLANN O'BRIEN
Loot, JOE ORTON
Ain't I a Woman?, SOJOURNER TRUTH
Noël Coward Diaries, NOËL COWARD
Dear Mr Eggnogge, THE *SPITTING IMAGE* BOOK
First They Came for the Jews, PASTOR NIEMOELLER

JOHN UPDIKE

1980

Death, terrors in childhood and a faint light glimmering in the darkness, John Updike in his programme pondered on these, and they have obviously been a refrain throughout all his life. As a child he saw the Bible as containing 'much dark matter. There was, to the small child, much hate, terror and abandonment in it.' He had not expected to find the hard face of God in the New Testament. He empathized with 'the timidity of the man who, entrusted with but one meagre talent, buried it in the ground for safe keeping.' He was shocked and tried to be illuminated 'dark as it was' – again that faint light. At the end he thanked the actors for their 'brilliant re-animation of the ghosts from my personal world of print'. John Updike somehow managed to combine an autobiography of his inner mind with a robustness much enjoyed by the audience.

The first poem which made an impression on me is this one. It frightened me. People in Pennsylvania believed in goblins and James Whitcomb Riley, a popular nineteenth-century poet from Indiana, reinforced that belief powerfully. I think that Miss Tate of the third grade used to read this poem to us; through it and the alarming reassurance of its refrain I did receive my first impression of poetry as something potentially powerful, with the peculiar power of rhyme and meter.

Little Orphant Annie
JAMES WHITCOMB RILEY

Little Orphant Annie's came to our house to stay,
An' wash the cups an' saucers up, an' brush the crumbs away,

An' shoo the chickens off the porch, an' dust the hearth an'
   sweep,
An' make the fire, an' bake the bread, an' earn her
   board-an'-keep;
An' all us other children, when the supper-things is done,
We set around the kitchen fire an' has the mostest fun
A-list'nin' to the witch-tales 'at Annie tells about,
An' the Gobble-uns 'at gits you
      Ef you
       Don't
        Watch
         Out!

Wunst they wuz a little boy wouldn't say his prayers, –
An' when he went to bed at night, away up-stairs,
His mammy heerd him holler, an' his daddy heerd him bawl,
An' when they turn't the kivvers down, he wuzn't there at all!
An' they seeked him in the rafter-room, an' cubby-hole, an'
   press,
An' seeked him up the chimbly-flue, an' ever'-wheres, I guess;
But all they ever found wuz thist his pants an' roundabout: –
An' the Gobble-uns'll git you
      Ef you
       Don't
        Watch
         Out!

An' one time a little girl 'ud allus laugh an' grin,
An' make fun of ever' one, an' all her blood-an'-kin;
An' wunst, when they was 'company', an' old folks wuz there,
She mocked 'em an' shocked 'em, an' said she didn't care!
An' thist as she kicked her heels, an' turn't to run an' hide,
They wuz two great big Black Things a-standin' by her side,
An' they snatched her through the ceilin' 'fore she knowed what
   she's about!
An' the Gobble-uns'll git you
      Ef you
       Don't
        Watch
         Out!

An' little Orphant Annie says, when the blaze is blue,
An' the lamp-wick sputters, an' the wind goes woo-oo,
An' you hear the crickets quit, an' the moon is gray,
An' the lightning'-bugs in dew is all squenched away, –
You better mind yer parunts, an' yer teachers fond an' dear,
An' churish them 'at loves you, an' dry the orphant's tear,
An' he'p the pore an' needy ones 'at clusters all about,
Er the Gobble-uns'll git you
Ef you
Don't
Watch
Out!

The next selection is also alarming. One is admonished as a child to read the classics without being told that the grim vision of the great writer might overwhelm a child's sensibility. In the middle of *Tom Sawyer*, which is urged upon fifth-grade children, there is a long episode in which Tom and his platonic girl friend, Becky, go into a cave and wander deeper and deeper – they come to a realm where there are no more initials scratched on the wall, no more candle stubs can be found and they become lost and it's very well described and very well felt. They wind up in the deep dark, the candle goes out, Becky curls up in a little passive ball and waits for death to come while Tom crawls up one limestone tunnel after another in an apparently hopeless search for the way out. He does indeed see at the end of a tunnel a bit of light, crawls toward it and comes out on the banks of the Mississippi, five miles beyond where they entered. The sequel of this horrifying episode is that the town, being an activist welfare-minded town, puts an iron gate over the mouth of the cave to prevent anything like this happening again. Tom is conveniently sent to sleep by the author for long enough to permit this to happen because when he wakes up he tells them that Injun Joe, a town outlaw, is in that cave also. At one point in this terrifying adventure Tom glimpsed Injun Joe holding a candle, so the townsfolk rush to the mouth of the cave.

Tom Sawyer
MARK TWAIN

When the cave door was unlocked, a sorrowful sight presented itself in the dim twilight of the place. Injun Joe lay stretched upon

194

the ground, dead, with his face close to the crack of the door, as if his longing eyes had been fixed, to the latest moment, upon the light and the cheer of the free world outside. Tom was touched, for he knew by his own experience how this wretch had suffered. His pity was moved, but nevertheless he felt an abounding sense of relief and security, now, which revealed to him in a degree which he had not fully appreciated before how vast a weight of dread had been lying upon him since the day he lifted his voice against this bloody-minded outcast.

Injun Joe's bowie-knife lay close by, its blade broken in two. The great foundation-beam of the door had been chipped and hacked through, with tedious labor; useless labor, too, it was, for the native rock formed a sill outside it, and upon that stubborn material the knife had wrought no effect; the only damage done was to the knife itself. But if there had been no stony obstruction there the labor would have been useless still, for if the beam had been wholly cut away Injun Joe could not have squeezed his body under the door, and he knew it. So he had only hacked that place in order to be doing something – in order to pass the weary time – in order to employ his tortured faculties. Ordinarily one could find a dozen bits of candle stuck around in the crevices of this vestibule, left there by tourists; but there were none now. The prisoner had searched them out and eaten them. He had also contrived to catch a few bats, and these, also, he had eaten, leaving only their claws. The poor unfortunate had starved to death. In one place, near at hand, a stalagmite had been slowly growing up from the ground for ages, builded by the water-drip from a stalactite overhead. The captive had broken off the stalagmite, and upon the stump had placed a stone, wherein he had scooped a shallow hollow to catch the precious drop that fell once in every three minutes with the dreary regularity of a clock-tick – a dessertspoonful once in four and twenty hours. That drop was falling when the Pyramids were new; when Troy fell; when the foundations of Rome were laid; when Christ was crucified; when the Conqueror created the British Empire; when Columbus sailed; when the massacre at Lexington was 'news'. It is falling now; it will still be falling when all these things shall have sunk down the afternoon of history, and the twilight of tradition, and been swallowed up in the thick night of oblivion.

Has everything a purpose and a mission? Did this drop fall patiently during five thousand years to be ready for this flitting human insect's need? And has it another important object to accomplish ten thousand years to come? No matter. It is many and many a year since the hapless half-breed scooped out the stone to catch the priceless drops, but to this day the tourist stares longest at that pathetic stone and that slow-dripping water when he comes to see the wonders of McDougal's cave. Injun Joe's cup stands first in the list of the cavern's marvels.

I went to college and while there majored in what was called English Lit. and my speciality was the seventeenth century – strange to say – and my speciality within that was poetry. It wasn't just that Eliot had made the metaphysicals chic; perhaps the same mind that used to delight in mystery novels was able to enjoy conceits elaborately developed. I've picked to represent this mass of literature a poem by John Donne.

A Valediction: of Weeping
JOHN DONNE

Let me pour forth
My tears before thy face, whilst I stay here,
For thy face coins them, and thy stamp they bear,
And by this mintage they are something worth,
For thus they be,
Pregnant of thee;
Fruits of much grief they are, emblems of more,
When a tear falls, that thou falls which it bore,
So thou and I are nothing then, when on a divers shore.

On a round ball
A workman hath copies by, can lay
An Europe, Afric, and an Asia,
And quickly make that, which was nothing, all,
So doth each tear,
Which thee doth wear,
A globe, yea world by that impression grow,
Till thy tears mixt with mine do overflow
This world, by waters sent from thee, my heaven dissolved so.

O more than Moon,
Draw not up seas to drown me in thy sphere,
Weep me not dead, in thine arms, but forbear
To touch the sea, what it may do too soon;
Let not the wind
Example find,
To do me more harm, than it purposeth;
Since thou and I sigh one another's breath,
Whoe'er sighs most, is cruellest, and hastes the other's death.

I discovered the English novelist, Henry Green, at about the same
time as I was taking in Wallace Stevens, and I was so struck by
their resemblance, one to another, that I wrote a poem about it.

They were both business men, both mandarins, both wrote a
kind of exquisiteist prose and poetry and both inspired love in
me. My poem was written, I think, when I was about twenty-five.
'An Imaginable Conference' it's called, with a subtitle 'Mr. Henry
Green, Industrialist and Mr. Wallace Stevens, Vice-President of
the Heartread Accident and Indemnity Company, meet in the
Course of Business'.

Exchanging gentle grips the men retire
Prolonged by courteous bumbling at the door,
Retreat to where a rare room deep
Exists on an odd floor, subtly carpeted,
The walls wear charts like chequered vests
And blotters ape the green of cricket fields.
Glass multiplies the pausing men to twice infinity
An inkstand of blue marble has been carven
No young girl's wrist is more discreetly veined.
An office boy, misplaced and slack, intrudes
Apologies, speaking without commas,
'Oh sorry sirs I thought'
Which signifies what wimbly wambly stuff it is
We seem to be made of.
Beyond the room a gander's son pure rhetoric ferments
Imbroglios of bloom.
The stone is so.
The peer confers in murmurings

With words select and Sunday soft
No more is known but rumour goes
That as they hatched the deal
Vistas of lilac waited their shrewd lids.

Readers: Eleanor Bron, Ed Bishop

Full Selection:
Genesis 37, THE BIBLE
St Matthew, THE BIBLE
Little Orphant Annie, JAMES WHITCOMB RILEY
Tom Sawyer, MARK TWAIN
The Owl Who Was God, JAMES THURBER
On the Vanity of Earthly Greatness, ARTHUR GUITERMAN
The Problem of the Green Capsule, JOHN DICKSON CARR
A Valediction: of Weeping, JOHN DONNE
Upon Julia's Clothes, ROBERT HERRICK
Upon Prew His Maid, ROBERT HERRICK
To Criticks, ROBERT HERRICK
Moby-Dick, HERMAN MELVILLE
Sunday Morning, WALLACE STEVENS
An Imaginable Conference, JOHN UPDIKE
Nothing, HENRY GREEN
Journals, SØREN KIERKEGAARD
On the Circuit, W. H. AUDEN

IAN WALLACE

1988

Ian Wallace is one of the nicest men in radio. I first worked with him over twenty years ago when I was a junior studio manager responsible for the spot effects – opening and shutting doors, rattling cups of tea, walking on gravel, etc. – for a series of 'Flying Doctor'. Not much of it remains with me save the memory of Bill Kerr on a ladder declaiming to a studio wall and of Ian Wallace playing the part, I think, of a Maori. In each episode of this masterpiece he had to sing a song in a ringing bass-baritone. After he had mellifluously thrown off a number called something like 'Tahiti Nooky' he confessed to me that he had learnt it the night before whilst watching television. Many years later I had the pleasure of producing him in a musical version of Oscar Wilde's The Selfish Giant *and, more recently, his 'With Great Pleasure'. Backstage he sang to us a little, his voice every bit as good as it had been all those years ago.*

I'm sure you've noticed that when interviewers ask any victim over a certain age about their childhood reading very many will reply, 'I read everything I could lay my hands on,' almost as though they feared that this exciting new found skill would be snatched away before the eager curiosity of youth could be satisfied.

My childhood reading filled in hours totally devoid of television for the simple reason that it hadn't been invented. There was the crystal set, but it provided programmes chosen for us by Sir John Reith rather than by popular demand. Even so I was a torch under the bedclothes reader as well.

199

I was born in London, the only child of Scots parents exiled by the needs of my father's business and being not a very robust child was frequently confined to bed with chest colds or tonsilitis – an unlikely start for an opera singer, but there you are. On these occasions my mother, undoubtedly an actress manqué, would deploy the full range of her suppressed histrionic talent to make me forget the alarming symptoms of bronchial asthma. I can still remember the thrill of anticipation as she embarked on the first page of Robert Louis Stevenson's *Treasure Island*.

Treasure Island
ROBERT LOUIS STEVENSON

Squire Trelawney, Dr. Livesey, and the rest of these gentlemen having asked me to write down the whole particulars about Treasure Island, from the beginning to the end, keeping nothing back, but the bearings of the island, and that only because there is still treasure not yet lifted, I take up my pen in the year of grace 17—, and go back to the time when my father kept the Admiral Benbow inn, and the brown old seaman, with the sabre cut, first took up his lodging under our roof.

I remember him as if it were yesterday, as he came plodding to the inn door, his sea-chest following behind him in a hand-barrow; a tall, strong, heavy, nut-brown man; tarry pigtail falling over the shoulders of his soiled blue coat; his hands ragged and scarred, with black, broken nails; and the sabre cut across one cheek, a dirty, livid white. I remember him looking round the cove and whistling to himself as he did so, and then breaking out in that old sea-song that he sang so often afterwards:

> 'Fifteen men on the dead man's chest –
> Yo-ho-ho, and a bottle of rum!'

in the high old tottering voice that seemed to have been tuned and broken at the capstan bars. Then he rapped on the door with a bit of a stick like a handspike that he carried, and when my father appeared, called roughly for a glass of rum. This, when it was brought to him, he drank slowly, like a connoisseur, lingering on the taste, and still looking about him at the cliffs and up at our signboard.

'This is a handy cove!' says he, at length, 'and a pleasant sittyated grog-shop. Much company, – mate?'

My father told him no – very little company, the more was the pity.

'Well then,' said he, 'this is the berth for me. – Here you matey,' he cried to the man who trundled the barrow; 'bring up alongside and help up my chest. I'll stay here a bit,' he continued. 'I'm a plain man; rum and bacon and eggs is what I want, and that head up there for to watch ships off. – What you mought call me? You mought call me captain. Oh, I see what you're at – there;' and he threw down three or four gold pieces on the threshold.

'You can tell me when I've worked through that,' says he, looking as fierce as a commander.

I had the good fortune to be sent to Charterhouse where we are this evening and where fifty years ago there was a collection of masters, so many of them characters in their own right that I could supply descriptions of at least twelve of them good enough for the police to issue identikit pictures. One, Frank Ives, introduced us to poetry, especially Victorian narrative verse and the romantics, reading for us with gusto and conviction. And this tough, wiry little man who also commanded the Officers' Training Corps was not embarrassed by his emotion even when, occasionally, he brushed away a tear. He was at his best where some histrionic effort was required as in Robert Browning's 'My Last Duchess'. The haughty, jealous, recently widowed Duke showing off one of his paintings to an emissary from a prospective new father-in-law was meat and drink to Frank.

My Last Duchess
ROBERT BROWNING

That's my last Duchess painted on the wall,
Looking as if she were alive. I call
That piece a wonder, now: Frà Pandolf's hands
Worked busily a day, and there she stands.
Will't please you sit and look at her? I said
'Frà Pandolf' by design, for never read
Strangers like you that pictured countenance,

The depth and passion of its earnest glance,
But to myself they turned (since none puts by
The curtain I have drawn for you, but I)
And seemed as if they would ask me, if they durst,
How such a glance came there; so, not the first
Are you to turn and ask thus. Sir 'twas not
Her husband's presence only, called that spot
Of joy into the Duchess' cheek: perhaps
Frà Pandolf chanced to say 'Her mantle laps
Over my lady's wrist too much,' or 'Paint
Must never hope to reproduce the faint
Half-flush that dies along her throat:' such stuff
Was courtesy, she thought, and cause enough
For calling up that spot of joy. She had
A heart – how shall I say? – too soon made glad,
Too easily impressed; she liked whate'er
She looked on, and her looks went everywhere.
Sir, 'twas all one! My favour at her breast,
The dropping of the daylight in the West,
The bough of cherries some officious fool
Broke in the orchard for her, the white mule
She rode with round the terrace – all and each
Would draw from her alike the approving speech,
Or blush, at least. She thanked men, – good! but thanked
Somehow – I know not how – as if she ranked
My gift of a nine-hundred-years-old name
With anybody's gift. Who'd stoop to blame
This sort of trifling? Even had you skill
In speech – (which I have not) – to make your will
Quite clear to such an one, and say, 'Just this
Or that in you disgusts me; here you miss,
Or there exceed the mark' – and if she let
Herself be lessoned so, nor plainly set
Her wits to yours, forsooth, and made excuse,
– E'en then would be some stooping; and I choose
Never to stoop. Oh sir, she smiled, no doubt,
Whene'er I passed her; but who passed without
Much the same smile? This grew; I gave commands;
Then all smiles stopped together. There she stands

As if alive. Will 't please you rise? We'll meet
The company below, then. I repeat,
The Count your master's known munificence
Is ample warrant that no just pretence
Of mine for dowry will be disallowed;
Though his fair daughter's self, as I avowed
At starting, is my object. Nay we'll go
Together down, sir. Notice Neptune, though,
Taming a sea-horse, thought a rarity,
Which Claus of Innsbruck cast in bronze for me!

One Scots versifier has given me considerable pleasure, William McGonagall, whose doggerel sincerely chronicled nineteenth-century triumphs and disasters and has provided subsequent generations with the delight of unconscious humour. Here are a few verses from one of my favourites.

The Humble Heroine
WILLIAM MCGONAGALL

'Twas at the Siege of Matagarda, during the Peninsular War,
That a Mrs. Reston for courage outshone any man there by far;
She was the wife of a Scottish soldier in Matagarda Fort,
And to attend her husband she there did resort.

And Captain Maclaine of the 94th did the whole of them
    command,
And the courage the men displayed was really grand;
Because they held Matagarda for fifty-four days,
Against o'er whelming numbers of the French – therefore they
    are worthy of praise.

There was one woman in the fort during those trying days,
A Mrs. Reston, who is worthy of great praise;
She acted like a ministering angel to the soldiers while there,
By helping them to fill sand-bags, it was her constant care.

Methinks I see a brave heroine carrying her child,
Whilst the bullets were falling around her, enough to drive her
    wild;

And bending over it to protect it from danger,
Because to war's alarms it was a stranger.

And while the shells shrieked around, and their fragments did
    shatter,
She was serving the men at the guns with wine and water;
And while the shot whistled around, her courage wasn't slack,
Because to the soldiers she carried sand-bags on her back.

A little drummer boy was told to fetch water from the well,
But he was afraid because the bullets from the enemy around it
    fell;
And the Doctor cried to the boy, Why are you standing there?
And Mrs. Reston said, Doctor, the bairn is feared, I do declare.

And she said, Give me the pail, laddie, I'll fetch the water,
Not fearing that the shot would her brains scatter;
And without a moment's hesitation she took the pail,
Whilst the shot whirred thick around her, yet her courage didn't
    fail.

So the French were beaten and were glad to run,
And the British for defeating them golden opinions have won;
All through brave Captain Maclaine and his heroes bold,
Likewise Mrs. Reston, whose name should be written in letters
    of gold.

Having set out to be an actor it was a great surprise to find that
those friends who counselled me to audition for an opera company were proved right. However, one of my early extra-operatic
activities was to take part in a dramatized version of Hilaire
Belloc's book *The Four Men* on a tour of Sussex towns and villages
to celebrate the Festival of Britain. We opened in Chichester and I
was billeted with the poet Robert Gittings and his wife Jo in a
nearby village. I arrived late on a still summer evening and we sat
silent by the open window until we were rewarded by their
resident nightingale. That was thirty-five years ago when we
were all a long way from that part of life when the shadowy
coastline of mortality is faintly discernible on the far horizon.
Robert sends his friends a poem every Christmas, but this one is
for a season hopefully still remote.

Imaginings
ROBERT GITTINGS

I go to all the places you once loved,
Everywhere lost. I see a smudge of red
Climbing the path ahead,
Reach it at burst of lung; it has not moved;
Only a picnic rag fluttering the bush,
Not your coat's scarlet. In the birdsong hush
I hear alone the tears I have to shed.

I go to all the valleys you once named,
Deep Combe, Half Moon, and silent Celtic Fields,
Names only. Nothing yields
Your voice to me, no whisper that exclaimed
As deer and fawn came trotting the long ride
With delicate printed track from side to side.
They go, and leave a grief that nothing shields,

The naked grief that keeps an open nerve
To casual promptings, sharp and unaware,
The cold form of the hare,
Empty reminders of the populous day
You made around you, and which shaped the way
We went through time in your unconscious care.

All these imaginings – if you should go
Before me! And if I should leave the first –
Each choice impossibly worst –
And you the one to take the upward, slow,
Trail through the woodland, O, I promise you,
With my pale, breathless, tenuous residue,
I shall be trying to reach you, though the heart burst.

Readers: Michael Williams, Jill Baker

Full Selection:
Parliament Hill Fields, JOHN BETJEMAN
Treasure Island, ROBERT LOUIS STEVENSON
My Last Duchess, ROBERT BROWNING

INDEX